Faith, Fatherhood & Food

A Decade of Personal Essays

By Ken Craig

©2019

Contents

Introduction

College was a formative time of my life. An era of learning – primarily *experiential* learning. The art of flirting. Sticking to a food budget by knowing the areas of campus where promotional food was often distributed. And sometimes, if I wasn't being careful, some learning actually happened in a classroom.

There were two lessons I learned at that time that led to the creation of this book.

The first: The thrill of sharing stories. If you have friends who are captivating storytellers, treasure them. Cuff yourself to them. Find out whatever dirt on them you can and blackmail them into being your friend forever. You cannot put a price on these friendships. To this day, one of my favorite things is to sit in a living room, delicious food in my lap, no time restrictions, and entertain each other with personal stories.

The second: Writing personal narratives. I received my Bachelor of Arts degree in advertising – which, at the time, at my college, required a minor in business or English. I chose English, because I wanted to eventually be the creative director at an ad agency, and also, I owned no suit jackets – which I suspected was mandatory for business minors, and for which I did zero research to confirm that suspicion.

Trying to complete my English minor, I signed up for a class called "Writing Your Personal History." A class offered by Don Norton. It was in this class that I was introduced to "The Personal Essay." This was a form where you write out a single life experience in a short, essay-style, story. And you can select whatever experiences you want – your earliest memory, your first kiss, your most embarrassing moment, etc.

For my first assignment, I wrote an essay about the time my dad forced me to go skydiving. Dr. Norton read my paper out loud to the class, and when he finished, he re-read his favorite line from the essay, turned to me, and said, "*How* did you come up with *that*?" I was completely surprised, flattered, and committed to writing more personal essays.

And now, years later, I have a collection of personal essays – or personal stories. Stories from different periods of my life, that I would share with you if we were swapping stories at lunch or in my living room, or at a party where I've cornered you and I won't let you leave until I tell you about the time I had to personally deliver my daughter because we didn't call the midwife in time.

And that is pretty much the format of this book. These are not chronological – so you may read a story early on where I state that I have eight children, and then later read a story where I claim to have five children. Before you call Child Protective Services, I did not sell three of my children. The date under the title of each story will give you an indication of the time frame and why some circumstances may be different.

Thank you for letting me share these stories with you! And if you're one of my children (which is most likely the case), I hope I haven't embarrassed you!

ALLOW MYSELF TO INTRODUCE OURSELVES

"The first few years, every nick that table absorbed, I took it personally. It was all I could see. The dent from a fork, the scratch from a skate blade, the ghost of someone's handwriting, pressed through a piece of paper. There were a lot of times I regretted not making that table out of oak. But as the years went by and the scars add-ed up ... the imperfections turned that table into something else. That's the thing about pine. It holds a lot of memories."

– Craig Morrison, *Still Mine*

Ten is a Magic Number

Written April 25, 2013

This is a photo of Katie and me in 1996, moments after we found out she was pregnant for the very first time. Nine months later, we had Abbie.

We had set the camera up on some makeshift pile of teetering books in our apartment, set the timer, and ran into position. It's an interesting moment. The photo itself seems to have captured us off guard, like we weren't quite ready when the timer went off. And when I look at this photo, it seems like a reflection of how I remember feeling in that instant. Close to Katie, not quite prepared, and not sure how the picture would turn out.

Katie was 21 years old, and I was 25. How could we possibly know how our picture would turn out? It's been 16 years now, and, metaphorically, the picture is still developing. But the development is exciting. It's interesting, detailed, and colorful.

Sometimes it's unexpected and imperfect. Most times it makes me smile. And I'm grateful for the people that show up as our family photo develops. I am privileged to know them. Including the newest one, who will be arriving in November.

Yep, Katie is pregnant with our 8th child.

Comedian Jim Gaffigan, who grew up in a family of six children and is now a father of five, once said, "Big families are like waterbed stores. They used to be everywhere, now they're just weird."

I don't know what the threshold is before one is considered A Large Family, but I do know that it's already been several years that we've been fielding that "Ah, nuts" look on the faces of waitresses, librarians, and people sitting behind us at the movies.

Once, while shopping at Costco (naturally), an employee actually watched our parade go by and queried, "Is this a school field trip?" Katie responded, "No. It's a family." (As if schools spend Family Home Evening at Costco.)

A good portion of the public gives me incredulous looks when I declare that I love having a big family; and I can see why. After all, I have consciously selected a lifestyle where nothing I own looks nice for very long. Not the couches, not the carpet, not my dress shirts, not our books, not the yard, not the computer keyboard, not the stair railing, and certainly not the car. My gosh, the car.

I suppose there is also a heightened level of inconvenience associated with having numerous children. I can't remember the last time I wasn't at least *kind of* tired. I've had to, for the most part, surrender to any form of timing or rhythm in scheduling life. Bedtime is sometime after 8 p.m. and before 10 p.m. Sports, church activities, piano lessons, Cub Scouts, and dinner are all strategically scheduled (by outside forces) to occur at the same time. And if you are supposed to be somewhere at 8:00 a.m., it doesn't matter if you start getting ready to leave the Tuesday before, you will not make it before 8:12 a.m., as you will get halfway there before you have to turn around and go back because somebody is not wearing shoes, or socks, or pants. And you just pray it is one of the children and not you.

Lucy, age 3, foot-fashion-forward and ready for the Primary Program at church.

But the frenzied mayhem and borderline lawlessness of the wild frontier known as Parents of a Large Brood is truly inspiring to me. Nothing makes me as happy as my family. Nobody makes me laugh more. Nobody makes me feel more loved. I never feel more centered than when I am doing something for the emotional, spiritual, mental, or physical well-being of my family. I am a better person because I get to be a dad to these eight souls.

Reader's Indigestion

Written September 17, 2007

I recently canceled my longtime subscription to *Reader's Digest*. Originally, we subscribed to this national treasure for two reasons: My wife grew up with it, so it was a bit of nostalgia for her, and I needed something to peruse whilst lounging in the bathroom.

I'm kidding of course. I haven't lounged in a bathroom in ages. Not since I've had children old enough to recognize that when Dad is in the restroom, he is trapped. They have a captive audience, and it's an opportunity to tell me the details of their day, get my opinion on their outfit, or – and I wish I were making this up – cram a drawing they made for me under the door, so I can compliment their artistic abilities.

Kid 1: (Paper appearing as if printing off a dot matrix. being wedged between the door and the floor) Daddy, I made this for you while you were at work!

Me: If you'll wait just a second, we can look at it together. Daddy just needs to finish reading about life-saving dental breakthroughs, and I'll be right out.

Kid 2: Dad, look, I'm waving at you! (Little fingers sticking out from under the door.)

Me: Yes, mm-hm, I'm waving back! Why don't you go see what your brother is doing?

Kid 3: (Faint knocking) Hi, Dad. I'm going to read you my book report on *Mr. Popper's Penguins*.

Me: Oh, why don't you go practice first, and then when I'm done, you'll be all ready.

Kid 4: Dad, can we play catch before dinner? I'll leave your glove here by the door.

Me: Katiiiiieee!

Katie: Kids, leave Daddy alone and come help me with dinner.

At any rate, the love affair with *Reader's Digest* has come to an end. It just sort of fizzled out. It seemed we had less and less in common. For example, "Life in These United States" is a *Reader's Digest* feature where people write in little personal experiences, recounting amusing anecdotes or misunderstandings or sound bites, so we can all chortle and say, "Oh, that is just like our little family/community/city/whatever. It sure is amusing, living in these United States."

My submission would be like this true story that happened on a recent car trip.

Daughter: Dad, can you think of another word for 'barf?'

Me: Barf?

Daughter: Yeah, we have 9 already, and we need 10. We have vomit, upchuck, puke…

Son: (Cutting Daughter off) Can we stop talking about barf….?

Wife: (Cutting Son off) That sounds like a great idea.

Son: (finishing)…and start talking about poop…?

My other observation is the celebrity interviews they do. Mercy, these people suck up to every celebrity they interview. No matter how controversial, offensive, or worse – boring – these celebrities are, *Reader's Digest* wants you to feel you can bring them home and introduce them to Mom.

If Charles Manson was on the cover, here are the questions you could expect to find *Reader's Digest* asking: "Of all the celebrities you've had the chance to meet and kill, which one impressed you the most?" "In between murders, aggravated assault, and larceny, you must have had a lot of down time. What kind of skills did you develop that have made you stronger today?" "You have claimed The Beatles were talking di-rectly to you in their song 'Helter Skelter.' What other musicians have influenced you since then?"

But what finally pushed me over the edge was when I called to cancel my subscription. They told me I couldn't. "Oh, no. We've already sent you issues you haven't paid for yet. You can't cancel now." That seemed a little dishonest to me. A little shady. A little "That's Outrageous!"

I immediately packed a suitcase and hatched a plan to fly directly out to Chappaqua, New York, publishing headquarters for the *Reader's Digest*. My plan was to march straight into to the president's office, knock on the door of his private bathroom, and cram a drawing under the door of what I was going to do to him if he didn't cancel my subscription. Now that's a ditty I'd like to see featured in "All in a Day's Work."

But instead I just called back, paid what I owed for the additional issues I had received, and canceled my subscription. Dear *Reader's Digest*, notify me when you have an article on that tenth barf synonym. Maybe then I'll renew my subscription.

Highs & Lows

Written May 5, 2011

A dinner ritual for our family is that we go around the table taking turns recounting our "highs and lows" for the day. You know, the best and worst things that took place that day. Our initial hope when we began this practice was that it might spur some lively conversation and provide some insight into how each child feels about their stage of life, current events, and of course, given them the opportunity to rat out their siblings' bad behavior and/or tell weird stories about their friends.

You might expect to hear something along the lines of, "Well, my 'highs' for the day included riding my bike, playing with Jo-Jo Marie – who told me that her dad passes gas when he's watching TV – and having a dance party with Abbie. My 'lows' were cleaning my room and also… when Tanner wouldn't let me play with his lightsaber!"

There have been some eyebrow-raising discussions, of course, but for the most part, I'm beginning to see a pattern develop.

Becca, who is 2 years old, generally starts the discussion by reminding us about it. "Mom! Dad! Highsandlows! Highsandlows!" (Most anything Becca says includes exclamation points.) Then Becca begins to give us not so much the stories of her "highs and lows," but an itinerary of what she's done that day. "Uhm, my highsandlows was, I eat breakfast…then I look at books…and my highandlows was, I played games with Connor…I made poops in the potty…and that's Lucy, and I kiss Lucy, and she's asleep, and that's all!"

Next is Tanner, age 5, who rather indignantly states, "Don't ask me what my highs and lows are. I've told you; don't ask me. Every day is just fine. I like all my days. I don't have 'highs and lows.'" Then Katie will try to jump-start it. "Well, what about when you played soccer in the backyard with Connor?" Then, with great conviction, "Yes. That was awesome. That was my high. But don't ask me anything else." Then Katie strategically mentions all the things he's done that day, item by item, and only then will Tanner admit that he had "highs and lows."

Then it's Roxanna's turn. She's 7. And as anticipated, Roxanna (possibly our pickiest eater) will look down at her plate and say, "Well my low is having to have two asparaguses…and kind of this salad, too… (then, moving her fork like a laser-pointer in a marketing presentation) … and my high is this chicken."

Connor, age 9. Connor is a little more diverse, except that his list invariably includes Star Wars or Legos. But if he has watched a movie that day, it will always be listed as a 'high.' No matter how terrible the movie. "My 'high' today was watching *The Berenstein Bears and the Messy Room*." Me: "No, it wasn't." "Yes, it was." "That could not have been your 'high.' Do we even own that movie?" "Yeah…I don't know where we got it. It's pretty lame. But that was my 'high!'"

Garren, age 11. Garren is at a magical age where he still thinks that doing anything with his dad is cool. Whatever we've done together that day, Garren will list it as one of his 'highs.' "My 'high' was picking weeds with dad in the front yard. Then a gang of bikers came by – you should have seen them – they got off their bikes and waved knives in our faces – they stole our minivan out of the driveway – they graffiti'd the house – they threw beer bottles at us – one of the bottles hit me in the head. I probably need stitches. And Dad and I were like, 'Whoa!' Those were my 'highs.'"

Abbie, age 13. Abbie will genuinely share her "highs and lows." Her dreams, her disappointments. Her hopes, her fears. But not her crushes. Some things are just not for public consumption.

And we mustn't forget Lucy, who is 2 weeks old and currently has no lows.

What are my highs and lows? My high is that my children will openly share their lives with me. My low is the thought that at someone else's dinner table, their child is sharing that "Tanner's dad passes gas while he watches TV."

THIS IS WHY WE CAN'T HAVE NICE THINGS

"All things on earth only exist in different stages of becoming garbage. Your home is a garbage-processing center where you buy new things, bring them into your house, and slowly crappify them over time."

– Jerry Seinfeld

Gettin' the Heck Outta Dodge

Written April 26, 2008

I have never felt defined by the car I drive.

My dad cured me of this when, on my 16th birthday, he gave me a 1976 Honda Civic that had been sitting idle in the garage since 1952. The original paint had faded (I'm assuming, since no self-respecting car should ever be that shade of orange), there was no air conditioning, no stereo, and the passenger seat was broken, so that the left half of the seat kind of fell to the side, letting the passenger rest on the driver's shoulder. This was perfect for dates, but not so great for my friend and customary passenger, Steve.

Anyway, being 16, I installed a stereo and the car was perfect. I couldn't care less about what anybody else was driving, or how I looked cruising through the high school parking lot listening to Beastie Boys with Steve nestled on my shoulder. In fact, I specifically remember one time seeing a guy get out of his Chevy Camaro in the parking lot and blasting from his car stereo for all the high school to hear, Lionel Richie's "Dancing on the Ceiling." I thought to myself, "How embarrassing for him. Truly, he's "(Nerdy) Like Sunday Morning." So clearly, to me, music was more defining of somebody's character than the car he drove.

And now, as an adult, I am equally disinterested in the car model I own. My criterion is that the vehicle be able to comfortably get me from one place to another as inexpensively as possible. Alas, one recent summer, our Dodge Caravan no longer performed this basic task, so I finally had to drive it out into the desert and shoot it.

We bought said Dodge Caravan when it had about 42,000 miles on it. At the time of death, it had 193,842 miles to its name. It had wanted to die months earlier, but our family just wouldn't let it.

The final hoorah for this poor van was a trip from Las Vegas, Nevada to Breckenridge, Colorado for a family reunion.

We left Vegas and headed north that fateful August morning. The Vegas sun was up so it was already 146 degrees. We got about three hours into the trip, just outside of Cedar City, Utah, when the air conditioning went out. It wasn't Las Vegas Hot, but it was still miserable. Hours later we were all sweaty, stinky, suffering from heat exhaustion and a little bit cranky. The stereo had gone out on the van several months prior to this trip – rendering the car useless for quite some time already – so we just drove in silence. Nobody was saying much to anybody, unless they were breathing threatening remarks about staying on their side of the seat or making eye contact for too long.

As we finally reached Breckenridge, the temperatures were bearable. However, this was the same time that the transmission decided to hiccup. Nothing dramatic, but it gave me pause for all of three seconds until I was immediately distracted by the fun and frivolity of family and outdoor recreation, wrapped up in a delightful climate. No sense worrying about the van. Who knows if we'll ever really need it again?

The fun ended, and all distractions ceased as five days later we prepared to journey back home. Coming out of Breckenridge, we stopped at a gas station, and, sensing more hiccups, I poured some transmission fluid into the van. Truth be known, I resented even spending that much money on this limping vehicle. I didn't want to put one more dime into this sucker. Not for the transmission, not for the air conditioning, not 25¢ to put air in the tire. Nothing. All I needed was to push this baby another ten hours, and then she could give up. I wanted her to coast right into our driveway and pass away, the way Johnny Depp's boat sank just as he stepped onto the pier in *Pirates of the Caribbean*.

I stood outside the van in that gas station parking lot, visually and emotionally taking in the risk directly in front of me. The air was still; the family already sweating. But I knew we could make it. We *had* to make it!

I made direct eye contact with the sun. He stared right back at me, unflinching. A particularly round tumbleweed blew by, past the gas pump, off into the vacant landscape. Somewhere in the distance, a dog barked. All life's trials had led me to this point.

I looked into the van and locked eyes with Katie. She pulled her sunglasses to the tip of her nose, stared blankly at me…and then with all the unspoken understanding of a couple married 16 years, she winced. She had my back.

I slid into the driver seat.

"Belts," I ordered.

"Locked," the kids responded in well-trained unison, like the command unit they are.

"Snacks," I gave the next order.

"Loaded," they responded.

"People, we're gonna hit this road *hard*, and we're gonna hit it *fast*." (I paused for dramatic effect, turned the key, and gave that pitiful beast of a vehicle a push on the gas.) "Let's *do* this!"

Three hours later, my pep talk was losing its shine, but I was still feeling pretty confident. The transmission seemed to be holding up and we were making good time. But then, somewhere in the vast wasteland that is western Colorado/eastern Utah, my three-year old daughter, Roxanna, started to complain about feeling nauseous.

"My tummy hurts!" she said.

"It's the heat, Sweetie," said my wife, Katie. "Have a drink of water."

"But it *really* hurts!" said Roxanna.

"Just hang on," said Katie.

"Baaaaaarrffffff!" said Roxanna.

This was no ordinary barf. This was a barf of epic proportions. This was the barf all other barfs hope to be when they grow up. To make matters worse, Roxanna had eaten an obscene amount of pizza before we left. To make matters even *more* worse, my oldest daughter was sitting in front of Roxanna, directly in the line of fire. To make matters even the *most* worse, it was 112 degrees, so we now had Barf Potpourri permeating the car for everyone to enjoy.

Katie climbed to the back of the van, holding out a towel for Roxanna to barf into for what seemed like longer than your average span of Child Vomit Time. There was nothing but freeway around. No towns, no rest stops, no gas stations, no off-ramps…nothing. So I kept barreling down the highway in search of a service station, or barring that, a cliff.

"I *told* you my tummy was hurting!" Roxanna said.

"WWWAAAAAAAAAAAHHHHHHH!" said my 20-month old, Tanner, who was sick to death of his car seat and was just happy to join in the anarchy.

"JUST WATCH YOUR DVD!" I suggested calmly to any children who weren't yakking up pizza.

"I can't SEE the DVD! I have pizza barf in my hair!" screamed Abbie. "This is the worst birthday ever!"

Finally, I saw a Shell gas station and convenience store. Out in the middle of nowhere, with no neighboring town, there was a Shell station. I didn't know where the employees were bused in from, and frankly, I didn't care.

I pulled off the freeway, behind this 18-Wheeler. But before the off-ramp ended, the truck lost a gi-normous tire, and I hit it. I mean, I hit it hard. The entire planet turned suddenly silent and, in slow motion and with just as much gravity, we clocked in the same airtime as the Apollo 13's flight around the moon. Houston…we definitely have a problem.

And as we limped into the gas station, I could hear something underneath the van, dragging on the ground.

I got out to take a look. And there was this thing hanging from the van. There were no fumes, no leaks or drips – just a dangly thing where no dangly thing should be. So, being the mechanic that I was, I knew exactly what do to.

"Where is your duct tape?" I asked the attendant.

"Over there," she half-pointed, putting out her cigar.

"And your Wet Wipes?"

"We don't have any."

I couldn't have heard her correctly.

"I'm sorry? You don't *what*?"

With piercing eyes, she silently looked up at me from her hunting magazine. Startled, I shuffled two feet back from her, knocking into a Hostess stand and bumping a rack of cupcakes onto the floor. I found myself unable to make eye contact with her, suddenly convinced she would stab me with the bathroom key if I didn't beat it, pronto.

I grabbed my duct tape and a bunch of ice cream bars for my desolate family, and then bolted for the parking lot with faith that I would see sunlight again and my death would not become some weird cautionary tale for Boy Scouts about how they should always be prepared and at least know the basics about car maintenance.

While Katie secured her place in Heaven by cleaning up the barf and the people covered in it, I channeled my inner-caveman and duct-taped the pipe hanging from the bottom of the van. All tidy and secure, we were on our way. We still had hours to go, and though there were moments of uncertainty with the transmission, the heat, the jerry-rigged pipe under the van and the likelihood of my losing the one final marble rolling around in my head, by the grace of Dodge manufacturing and the longest prayer I've ever offered, we somehow made it safely into our driveway.

Once I hoisted every last body out of the van and into their bed, I went back outside and made my peace with that ol' Dodge. Her time had come. The next day, we gave her to a mechanic-friend of ours to fix up and sell for whatever he could get. I find myself hopeful that she's still around town somewhere, doing some good for somebody else. Our time with her is over now, but she'll always have our love ... our love ... our "Endless Love."

Midwife at the Oasis

Written December 1, 2013

December 2013

If you are just tuning into this program, I would like to bring up something that will more than likely make you think twice about where you are going to sit once you are visiting us inside this here Casa de los Craigs: We homebirth.

Yep, we have eight children, and seven of them were born at home. Two on two different couches, two on a bed, and three on a toilet. Yes, we employ the services of a midwife. Margie the Midwife, if you are going to press me for details. And yes, the toilet births were not intentional, and yes, the midwife wasn't here for two of them, and yes, it was totally our fault for not calling her at the appropriate time.

Actually, this is probably more information than any of you would care to know. Unless you are partial to words like "afterbirth," "placenta," "mucus plug," or "meconium." (Don't even look up that last word. Basically, it's "uter-poo.") But over the years, many people have wondered why we even considered using a midwife in the first place. Did we have a bad experience with a doctor? Do we not have insurance? Did we want to plant the placenta in the backyard and see what magically blossomed? Are we only a year out from moving to northern Idaho and living in a compound? Are we hippies? Does Katie shave her legs and/or armpits and is Ken growing his own crop of hemp?

See how quickly you got there? "Oh, the Craigs homebirth? I had no idea they were hillbillies."

The answer to your inquiring questions is this: maybe.

No, not really. Really, it all began when Katie was three months pregnant with Abbie, our first child, and suggested she would like to explore the possibility of using a midwife. I laughed and laughed and laughed…and laughed…but then I noticed she wasn't laughing. Then it got awkwardly silent. Then I cleared my throat, squinted as I pretended to look out the window, and told her how I thought we should grow some hemp in the backyard.

Truthfully, my knee-jerk reaction was to not entertain this idea for even a nanosecond. This stemmed directly out of me having no idea what using a midwife meant, but assuming it involved angry women posing as doctors who would try to exclude me from being involved in the birth of my baby. I also pictured large, Swedish women coming into our home with some medieval tools and a pot of hot water, instructing Katie to get up on the kitchen table and start pushing.

But in a still and tranquil moment one night, Katie quietly explained to me that she had a desire to experience birth naturally and she knew midwives would be supportive of that; and that she liked the idea of this personalized, nurturing care that would be more innate with a midwife than with a doctor who would not be standing by your side for the entire experience. It wasn't the first or last time that Katie used sense and quiet moments to convince me to do something that first appeared to me as suspect. She's sneaky that way.

Introducing Abbie. August 8, 1997

With Abbie, our first child, our foray into midwifery still included a hospital. This helped me ease into the midwife idea. I took comfort in the fact that if anything went horribly wrong, there were teams of surgeons, legions of medical instruments, and a cafeteria with cold cereal. (I like to snack on comfort foods in times of crisis.) So, for this particular high-wire act, we still had plenty of safety nets underneath us.

Whatever midwife reservations I had held on to leading up to Abbie's birth, they quickly disappeared after her delivery. Katie's labor lasted upwards of 40 exhausting hours, due to Abbie being posterior. Those long, painful hours still involved a strong heartbeat for the baby the entire time, plus regular, consistent contractions for Katie. They also included several walks, small meals, a viewing of *Groundhog Day*, a hot bath for Katie, zero naps, some vomiting (mostly from Katie, as she entered the transition stage), lots of shoulder shrugging from me, a million prayers (or one constant prayer), and wonderful midwives who supported Katie in every decision. There was no pressure for medical intervention or to even take drugs. (For Katie, I mean. It was a different story for me, as these midwives kept pressuring me to take all manner of hallucinogens. I think. I can't remember very clearly. I hadn't slept in over 48 hours.)

With this remarkable experience now logged away, we then moved to Las Vegas to start my post-college career. This is where we met Margie the Midwife, and with her on board, our second child, Garren, was born in our Las Vegas apartment, on our Futon.

At this point you're saying to yourself, "Futons aren't comfortable for sleeping on, sitting on, or even lifting to turn it from a couch into a bed – why on earth would you birth on one!?"

Well, because the kitchen table was still full of dishes from dinner. Not really. But although the old stereotypes were no longer registering with me, having a home birth wasn't exactly on our radar. Of course, living in Las Vegas and owning a Futon were never on our radar, either. You just can't predict everything, people.

We couldn't find a practice of certified nurse midwives, like we'd found in Utah, so we began looking at the option of a homebirth with a home-birth midwife. The hospital setting was more reassuring to me. Like it was *kind of* homebirthing...but with a net. (Which would probably still be more comfortable than birthing with a Futon.)

I act like it was this natural and carefree transition, but until we met Margie the Midwife, I was slightly unnerved. I would time how long it took me to drive from our apartment to the hospital, and I would try different routes. You know, in case of an emergency. Like an arm coming out before a head. Or like me freaking out. But after we met Margie, I had all the confidence in the world in her. I already had all the confidence in the world in Katie. So, I started to accept that this would be a really neat, really new experience. And Garren's birth then became our foray into homebirthing. And that's the way all of our children since Garren have been born. Including Roxanna and Becca ... who were both born before Margie arrived at our house to deliver them.

Introducing Roxanna. September 3, 2003.

On the morning of Roxanna's birth, Katie woke me up at 4:45 a.m. My first thought was that Katie was waking me up for TV sensation "That's Cat," but then I realized it was 2003. That stupid VH1's "I Love the 70s" episode from the night before was messing with my mind. Katie told me she had been awake for about an hour with some contractions that weren't horrible but were strong enough that they had woken her up. We called Margie the Midwife. Margie asked if we wanted her to come over to our house immediately. I looked up and saw Katie walk-ing around the room. She was casual and witty and not burdened by the contractions. We decided Margie didn't need to come yet, but we wanted to let her know that something was starting.

We crawled back into bed, and actually fell back asleep. And when I say "we," I totally mean "me." Katie fell asleep, then woke up to con-tractions, then went back to sleep, then woke up for contractions, then went back to sleep. You see the pattern. At about 7:00 a.m. we got out of bed. My mom was making breakfast for the kids, and we were hanging out in the bedroom, working through contractions with Katie breath-ing, and me holding her, or rubbing her back, or letting her hang on me.

We worked through the contractions for a while. I would help Katie work through one, then run to get something done, then come run-ning back for the next one, then run to get something done. You see the pattern. I started to notice my time for getting things done grew shorter and shorter, until Katie was leaving me practically no time to do anything, which is extremely rude, and I made a mental note to bring this up to her later, once our routine was back to normal.

I decided I'd time Katie's contractions to see if they were as close as I was thinking. And they were. A minute and a half long, only two minutes apart. They were right on top of each other. This usually means the Transition Stage has arrived, and then you start pushing. (And by "you," I totally mean "the mother.")

I told Katie how long her contractions were. Her comment was, "That's impossible. Look at me – I'm too chipper. I'm happy, I'm fine, I'm even a little bit sassy." She had a point, but I called Margie anyway. "Margie," says I, "Why don't you come on over for the party. Katie's says her contractions aren't really hard yet, but they are pretty close, and I'm sure we're on our way." "Okay," she said, "I'm going to throw some clothes on and I'll jump in the car." I appreciated knowing she would be dressed when she arrived.

Katie had decided to go to the bathroom, and then she would venture out of our bedroom for some breakfast. I hung up the phone to go check on Katie, and as I did, I heard, "Keeeeeennnnn!" This was a familiar yell. I had heard it at least three times before, with the birth of each of our children. I went running in. Katie looked up at me, from her location on the toilet, and in full confidence said, "I have to push."

Ah, nuts. I called Margie back and said, "Katie needs to push." I suppose I was hoping that Margie owned the DeLorean from *Back to the Future* and would be able to arrive immediately, if not five minutes ago. Margie shot back, "Oh, tell her not to push." Thanks, Margie. Katie's on the brink of delivering, and I'm going back in with "Margie says not to push."

"Margie says not to push," I told Katie. Katie looked up at me like she was wondering when I had started drinking in the mornings. Then there was a large gush of water. It was Katie's. The expression on Katie's face was telling me this was IT. I had seen it before and I knew this was it. I knelt down and had Katie scoot to the edge of the toilet and lean back. There was the baby's head. Not just a sliver of it, but the entire top of the head. At this point, it seemed it didn't matter if Katie pushed or not, the baby was coming out.

Katie seemed calm, and I think more than anything, that is what helped me be calm. I told Katie *I* was ready and that *she* could push when she was ready. She pushed once, and the head came right out, no problem. I put my hand on it to guide it out and waited for Katie to push again. Katie kind of panted and re-evaluated the situation. I told Katie that it seemed the baby's shoulders might be a bit stuck. Katie stood up, hunched over my shoulder and pushed again. The baby came right out into my arms.

Katie's mom stepped in with a towel and we wrapped up the baby and handed it to Katie, still sitting on the potty. I peeked under the towel and announced, "It's a girl!" Smiling and sighing, Katie echoed, "It's a girl!" Katie looked beautiful and powerful and kind. She looked incredible. I had the camera right there, so I took a photo of her. One of my most favorite photos ever taken of Katie.

I handed the baby to Katie's mom and helped Katie over to the bed. I set out some pads on the bed and she sat down. Katie's mom cleaned off the baby and brought her over to the bed. She nursed right away, perfectly.

Margie called from the road, stuck behind a car accident, and asked if everything was okay and when I said we were great, she told me to go ahead and cut the cord. I clamped it, an inch from the belly button, then cut it. We cleaned everything up, got Katie something to drink, and sat in complete amazement at what we had just done, all on our own.

Margie arrived. She weighed the baby and checked Katie to make sure she was okay. Everything was fine. To me, everything was more than fine. That is, for another five years, until almost the exact same thing happened again.

Allow Me to Introduce Rebecca. June 29, 2008.

Ladies and gentlemen, do you have trouble with guests who have over-stayed their welcome? Do you have company that just refuses to leave? Well, grab a pencil and jot this down. I have three little magic words that will clear your house faster than "I just tooted." Ready? "My water broke." (I learned yesterday, however, that this works equally well on guests that you are *not* trying to get rid of.)

If you've heard the birth story of our fourth child, Roxanna, this story is going to sound faintly familiar to you. The thought may even cross your mind that we must have wanted to do it this way on purpose. But then you might want to check your Crazy Pills prescription, because nobody would want to do it this way again on purpose. We even made a most concerted effort with our fifth child, Tanner, to make sure that it in fact *didn't* happen that way again. Plus, why would anybody consciously decide to pay for the loving care of a midwife, and then not invite them to come over for the love and care? And then why would you do that twice?! That's like experiencing a very unique movie, and realizing it was certainly a once-in-an-odd-lifetime experience, and then finding out there is an unnecessary sequel. (*Weekend at Bernie's II*, I'm looking in your direction.)

Well, it all started with a single contraction on Friday night. I was on my way to a "Weird Al" Yankovic concert with some of my other home-nerds, so you can imagine my relief when Katie said she was sure it was nothing and gave me the green light to rock on with Al and his accordion. (Speaking of once-in-a-lifetime odd experiences, I had seen Mr. Yankovic in concert in 1987 and had assumed that would be the only time. So, I should have seen this as a sign. But I was too busy wondering how My Man Weird is able to do so many costume changes in one concert. The man is truly an artist, clearly dedicated to his craft.)

True to her word, Katie had no other contractions. Until Saturday morning. Yes, beginning around 6:30 a.m. Katie started having extremely mild and completely irregular contractions. This continued through the early afternoon, when some friends/former college roommates of ours who were in town for the weekend brought lunch over.

Katie was feeling so great, she was able to be social and casual and showed no signs of ever being uncomfortable. She would still have the occasional contraction, but these were the most gentle and docile contractions ever recorded, according to Katie. The contractions weren't getting any harder, they weren't getting any closer, they didn't seem to be progressing at all! *I* could have had these contractions, and I have a very low tolerance for pain. (I also have a low tolerance for large crowds of Weird Al fans, it turns out. But this isn't about me. Or the fans.)

Around 2:30 p.m. Katie slipped into the downstairs bathroom just to tinkle. The rest of us were on the couches, chatting. Suddenly, Katie called for me. "Can you come in here for a second?" Normally, we don't invite each other into the bathroom when we're taking care of business, so this got my attention, as well as the attention of our guests.

I tried to open the door, but it was locked. "Can you unlock the door?" I asked.

"Nope," she answered.

"Well, we're going to get going!" said our college friends, leaping from the couch to gather their kids from upstairs, and, in the process, easily breaking the Olympic qualifying time for the track and field hurdles.

I grabbed a tool, picked the lock and opened the door to see my cute, sweet wife nestled in on the toilet. "My water broke," she said. "I need pads and dry clothes."

I retrieved the materials from upstairs, but I was actually quite casual about it because while Katie seemed energized that things were finally moving, she didn't seem overly anxious or concerned about the immediate moment we were in.

I walked back into the bathroom with her stuff and she said, "Why don't we call the Midwife. I think we're going to have this baby tonight." Now, our standard go-to Midwife that we have used for our last four children is Margie. Margie is wonderful. Margie knows her stuff. Margie makes you feel at ease.

Margie was on a cruise in the Bahamas.

But we had three back-up midwives to select from.

"Sounds good," I said. "I'll call one of the backup midwives. Did you want to say goodbye to the Muirs? They're leaving now."

"Uhm…no. If I get up, I just know I'll have a contraction."

I left the bathroom, said goodbye to the Muirs (who had already loaded their car), and was walking over to the phone to call a midwife when I heard Katie yell for me again. This was a different yell. This was a familiar yell. This was a "For the love of heaven, get in here and catch this baby" yell.

I opened the bathroom door, this time to find Katie pushing out a baby. Katie's head was down, her eyes closed, her arms stretched around her front with her hands holding the bottom of her stomach. She seemed remarkably peaceful. Focused. I have never known anybody to be able to understand their body like Katie. The room seemed entirely still and silent.

She looked up at me and said, "Tell me it's a head." This was a legitimate concern, because if it was a bum, a leg, or anything but a head, we were up an afterbirth creek, without a paddle.

I dropped down on my knees and saw the head out, just above the eyes. "It's a head," I said. "Are you ready?"

Katie started pushing again and the head came out. She pushed some more. "Is it further out?" she asked.

"No. Still just the head."

She pushed some more.

"I can see a shoulder, here it comes."

And she slipped right into my arms. She was covered in vernix, and now I was too. I held her so close because I thought she was going to slip-slide right out of my hands. She wasn't crying at all. I couldn't believe I was holding her. It felt as if we had waited so long for her.

It was 2:36 p.m., and all of our kids were peering from behind the bathroom door at this point, wanting to see what was going on. They came in to see her, and everybody crowded around her, except Tanner, the 2-year old, who had a very concerned look on his face. After he saw that Katie was okay, he seemed fine with the situation.

We called our friend and neighbor, Jonelle, who has been to a number of births. We knew she wouldn't freak out at being up to her ankles in … stuff. With the baby in Katie's arms, the placenta in a bucket, and Chux pads on the couch, Jonelle came over and helped me move Katie from the bathroom to the living room.

Katie sat down on the couch and started nursing the baby right away. We cut the cord and called the backup midwife, but she was with another woman who was laboring. We called the second backup, and she was in Boulder City with another woman who was laboring. (Which, honestly, how long does it take? If they are like Katie, we should have had a midwife arriving in about 15 minutes.) But she sent her apprentice over. The apprentice showed up about two hours after the birth. We sat there for two hours like it was the most normal, Saturday afternoon thing to do.

When the Apprentice arrived, she weighed the baby. According to the scale, she was 16 pounds. According to the Apprentice, the scale must be broken. We had Abbie stand on a normal scale, and then handed her the baby, and then figured the difference, which is about 10 lbs. and … some ounces.

We've named her Rebecca. (We call her Becca). She is lovely. I adore the smell of her newborn head and sweet breath. I love her dark eyes and quiet nature. As always, I am absolutely and, in every respect, overcome with wonder at Katie. She is powerful, soft, and warm. She is beautiful, secure, and poised. I wonder if we should have named the baby after her incredible mother. Or we could have named her "Weird Al"berta Craig.

All American Wife Swapping

Written December 16, 2006

If we're laying our cards out on the table, I should tell you that my wife and I homeschool our children. Or more precisely, *she* homeschools the kids, and I try not to muss it up. So far, so good. Our kids are intelligent, socially mature, inquisitive, verbal, well-bathed human beings. In other words, these aren't the children your weird neighbor was homeschooling circa 1976.

Having said that, we recognize that there is still a stereotype afloat regarding homeschooling. But we also have many good friends who homeschool their children, and together, we are going to change the world's perception – one well-adjusted, clothes-matching, non-snotnosed homeschooler at a time.

I bring this up because recently we received an email from ABC Television's very special show, *Wife Swap*, asking if we would be interested in participating as a featured family on this program. If you are like me, you have never seen a single episode of this show, but you're able to take one look at the show's title and immediately conclude that this is nothing less than stellar, highbrow television at its reality best.

The email we received actually possessed the intestinal fortitude to suggest that this show was nothing short of a miracle, healing families from coast to coast. That really, the timer has been turned on, and your family's success is living on borrowed time without regularly tuning into this insightful, family-saving program. Here are a couple of lines from the email:

The wives from these two families exchange husbands, children and lives (but not bedrooms) to discover just what it's like to live another woman's life. It's a mind-blowing experiment that often ends up changing their lives forever.

The reason we were contacted was because we are a homeschooling family, and this is an upcoming theme on the series. The email said, "In addition to homeschooling, tell us something about your family that you think would be interesting."

Oh, they had thrown down the gauntlet now. But, please. You're messing with the wrong guy. I knew exactly what they wanted to hear. It is obvious a show like this thrives on the three C's: Chaos, contention, and contractions.

"My wife and I have five children. We are also members of The Church of Jesus Christ of Latter-day Saints, so we are very religious. And my wife also births our children at home."

The phone rang within two hours. It was Michelle, with *Wife Swap*, and she was wondering if we could tell her a little more about ourselves. I think the first thing we shared with her at that point was that we weren't really interested in going any further with this.

She then told us it paid $20,000 for six days of filming. Which sounds like a lot of money, until you consider what you are allowing them to do. The show obviously moves along due in large part to the second C (contention). And to build contention, you need two families with completely different sets of values, beliefs, habits, hygiene, and affinity for bawdy stories. In other words, the Brady Bunch versus the Al & Peg Bundy Bunch.

We told Michelle she could pass our name along to the next level of screening, but that we would most likely not be interested. I get the heebie-jeebies when I think of a complete stranger watching over my children all day. But even more terrifying…what if we were the Bundys…and the other family was the Bradys? What if WE were the freaks?!

The Circus Is in Town

Written January 26, 2012

When I look back over my life up to this point, there is a non-short list of moments when I realize, "Oh. I'm *that* guy."

Completely snubbing the salad bar at a buffet so I can put those calories to better use by enjoying a third dessert? Yes. I'm that guy.

Staying up late watching a movie on TV that I already own on DVD and could watch at a reasonable hour? Yep. I'm that guy.

Waxing my face so I don't have to shave so often? Yes. Unfortunately, I am that guy. (Well, I was that guy on one, single occasion.)

And finally … owning a 12-passenger van just so my family can legally fit in the same car? Somehow…I am now *that* guy.

It's true. The Craig family has been relegated to driving what is essentially a bus. Apparently, we as a civilization agreed to let the automobile industry define "an acceptable family size" in this here country of ours. And evidently, that number is less than nine.

"Oh," Normal Car Designers say, "You've decided on having seven children? Well, guess what. You no longer fit in a standard minivan, you hippy freaks. Congratulations on being a spectacle. Please select a vehicle from our Nonconformist Line of Automobiles."

So, yeah, we are now that family. You know the one. You tell stories about them from when you were young. "Oh, man. There was this one family in our ward/neighborhood/trailer park/compound that was so big; they had to travel in a bus!"

But you know what? I fully embrace it. There are far more pros than cons in owning a vehicle that may or may not require a commercial license to drive.

Pros:

The fact that our family needs a vehicle this big means I have at least eight best friends and we now can go everywhere together.

I will never again have to set up a tent when "camping."

There is actually so much room on the benches that I have yet to hear "Will you stop touching me?!"

I will never lose it in a packed parking lot.

Soon I will be able to teach the kids "van surfing," as seen in the 1985 Michael J. Fox blockbuster, *Teen Wolf.*

At Halloween Trunk or Treats, we have enough room to make a spook alley right in our van!

For youth activities at church, the teenagers actually think it's cool to get to ride in a vehicle so big! Popularity! (Winning!)

You feel taller, and a little more regal, than everyone else on the road.

I think this summer I will try driving it around the neighborhood to sell ice cream from it.

There is enough space between the front and back that Katie and I can have private conversations!

On "date night," Katie and I can take the van out, find a nice quiet spot, lie down on the bench, and ... take a nap!

Cons:

When Katie wants to read to the kids (which she generally does on road trips), she has to use a megaphone for the kids in the back to hear.

Each time I fill the gas tank I think, "And now one less child gets to go to college."

P.S. Did I really just have a family photo shoot in front of our van? Yep. I'm that guy.

LOVE & OTHER IMPROVISATIONS

"You don't love someone for their looks, or their clothes, or for their fancy car, but because they sing a song only you can hear."

— Oscar Wilde

The Reason for the Season

Written August 3, 2009

I won't say that I knew I was going to marry Katie Fillmore the first time I met her. But I knew something was happening.

Let me back up.

Katie and I met in college as members of The Garrens Comedy Troupe, an improv and sketch comedy troupe. In fact, our first conversation took place in an improv where she was a 1950s homemaker and I was Droopy the Dog. Hilarity ensued.

You know, typical love story. Boy gets an audience suggestion for an occupation, girl asks for an annoying personal habit, and a scene is created. Boy asks girl what she's doing Friday night, girl has creative excuse for appearing busy ("The aliens are bestowing my super powers upon me on Friday, and they'll be so upset if I stand them up again"). Boy is persistent, girl's interest is piqued…a marriage is created.

Eight months before meeting Katie I was a founding member of The Garrens Comedy Troupe. We were the first improvisational and sketch comedy group to ever grace the land of Brigham Young University.

It was January 1993. It was the year of *Schindler's List*, civil war in Afghanistan, and the dissolution of Slovakia and the Czech Republic. So, as you can see, the world was rife with hilarity already! As a society we were infatuated with *Jurassic Park* and Eddie Vedder's reality-biting plaid, flannel fashion. Also, Whitney Houston would not shut up about how she would always love us.

Joining The Garrens Comedy Troupe terrified me, as I had not previously been much of a performer. But on a particular wintry day, my roommate and yours, Lincoln Hoppe, had seen a flier on campus, wherein some hooligan named Eric D. Snider was holding auditions so he could convince a couple of chumps to join him in starting a comedy troupe. Lincoln was thrilled with the idea. He was less thrilled with my openly mocking him for suggesting we go audition. (And less thrilled even further when he opened the fridge to discover I had not only drunk the last of his personal stash of Minute Maid, but put the empty pitcher back in the fridge for him to stumble upon. And you don't get those kinds of details in a story unless it's true.)

Don't get me wrong. In theory, I loved the idea of writing sketches and performing them. In theory, I also loved the idea of getting up in front of a crowd of people and not pooping my pants. So, you keep to your theories, and I'll keep to my unsoiled pants, and round n' round the world will go.

Well, we both auditioned and became part of BYU history that year by becoming members of The Garrens. The two of us, plus seven more mirthful souls. Our popularity soared! Between the hours of 7 p.m. and 10 p.m. on most Friday nights, at the Jesse Knight Humanities Building on BYU campus, to a crowd that was willing to pay $1 each to see us, we were practically celebrities! And then Winter Semester ended. And some of the cast members left to seek their fortune and fame by becoming Latter-day Saint missionaries. So, we held auditions to fill their spots.

And in late August of 1993 I sat in the back of that same room in the JKHB building with about five other members of The Garrens; watching for talent, energy, and which girls would most likely date us if we let them in the troupe. (I'm 70% kidding.)

Enter Katie Fillmore, center stage.

But I hadn't seen her yet.

In the back of this darkened theater room I was squinting at my pad of paper as I was still noting some detailed, astute, professor-like observations regarding the previous auditioning individual. "Not that funny," I wrote.

For her audition, we had placed Katie in an improvisation with Natalie (a current Garrens' member), wherein they had both been summoned to the high school principal's office and were sitting next to each other in anticipation. Natalie was an angst-y, angry hard rocker and Katie was a cheerleader. I'd heard the scene start, but I was still focused on my notes, and hadn't yet turned my attention to the stage.

Finally, I looked up. There, in all her glory, was my wife. Not yet. But in less than two years, she would change my life and make it better than I deserved.

I could not stop watching her.

The first thing I noticed was her eyes. And though I've never asked, I assume to this day that is the first thing anybody notices about Katie. It's not the color. It's not the lashes. It's the light. Those eyes are windows into what makes Katie…Katie. Her very essence. Her personality emanates out her eyes. I looked in those eyes and knew immediately she was a happy and kind spirit. Not just for the fleeting moment, but in her core.

She was wearing a yellow shirt, 1993 jeans, white sneakers, and a huge-normous smile. She was a force to be reckoned with, but not assuming. She didn't try to take over the stage but had a confidence in what she was doing. And she was hilarious. A 5'2" ball of energy and enthusiasm and wit and adorableness.

It wasn't love at first sight in any kind of formulaic way. I didn't think, "One day I will marry her." I didn't think, "Roll the montage sequence, we're in love." But it wouldn't be truthful to say it was *nothing*, either. It was *something*. Something extremely, profoundly deep, deep, deep in my soul reacted to Katie. Almost chemically. Like I could feel a physical change. Some trace part of me recognized her. Or was drawn out to her. Or something. I didn't know what it was in that moment. But I did know she would be in The Garrens. Her audition alone was outstanding; but even more, I could just sense she would be a part of my life. Even for just a season. Thankfully, though, it's been much longer.

Below is the first documented photo of Katie and me. It was right after a Garrens' show. That's me in the pink/red shirt, and that is Katie next to me. And who's that she's looking at? Is it the camera? No, it's ME! The flirting had begun.

If You Like Me, Check This Box

Written August 8, 2009

I was an advertising major in college. I wanted to write commercials for radio and television. My goal was to one day work at a large ad firm in Los Angeles, Chicago, New York, or San Luis Obispo. (I don't think there are any large agencies in San Luis Obispo, but, 1. I adore little beach towns, and 2. Don't you kind of giggle when you say, "San Luis Obispo?" Me too.)

In my dreams, I would have a little office with a window view of the ocean, an oversized poster of *The Joshua Tree* hanging on my wall, a mini-freezer filled with ice cream, and one of those little basketball hoops rigged atop a little wastebasket for the ultimate cliché of the tortured writer who rips scarcely touched paper with half-written ideas on it out of the typewriter, wads it up into a ball, and throws it at the wastebasket. (Camera cuts to the wastebasket, with nary a single wadded-up piece of paper inside, but about 23 wads peppered around the outside of the basket.) Also, everyone else in the office would give me a hard time for still using a typewriter in this day and age.

In an effort to stay true to my art form of writing, and to completely avoid developing any business savvy, I took only one business class in college. It was held in a stadium-seat classroom with hundreds of savvy business students and me and my roommate/fellow dreamer/future commercial writing partner – Lincoln.

We always sat in the front row. I don't know why we sat there. Maybe because we felt out of place with all the snooty business students. What with their briefcases, collared shirts, and large brains. It seemed like the average age in the classroom was 42, and I was at all times slightly uncomfortable, like somebody might stand, call my bluff, and demand my dismissal from this and any business classes. "Pardon me, Mr. Professor, your Honor, but I object to this hoodlum occupying a coveted seat in the front row of this, your stadium classroom. Furthermore, I submit that he has neither the inclination nor the maturation or substantiation for comprehending the volumes of wise and insightful tutorials you have prepared for us, your insatiable business students. Plus, I heard him make a fart joke when he walked into class today."

But I remained dutiful in attending my big business class. After all, I'd paid for it, I needed the credits to graduate … and my future wife, Katie Fillmore, happened to have a class in that same building, about half an hour after my class had started.

And then she started this little tradition that I adored.

About 25 minutes into every class, I would receive a love note from Katie. As if we were in junior high. They were always sweet and thoughtful, but my favorite part was that she would write the note, fold it up, and on the outside of the paper write: "Pass this note to the handsome, dark-haired man on the front row named 'Ken.'"

She would then sneak in the door of this monstrous classroom, tap the suit in the last row, at the top of the stadium-seating structure, and hand him the note. The guy would read the instructions to pass it down, and he would hand it to the guy in front of him. Down and down. Down and down. Down something like 36 rows of seats the note would go, until somebody would tap me on the shoulder and hand me the note.

Now, we had been dating several months at this point, and I think Katie truly loved me. I think she knew I appreciated getting these little notes. But somewhere in Katie's psyche, I think she also got the biggest kick out of this little phenomenon. That amidst all the no-nonsense attitudes of these business students, who would just as quickly clock you with their Franklin Planners as shoot you a dirty look for disturbing them during a business lecture, she could single-handedly reduce them to schoolyard behavior in three seconds flat. Inherent in everyone who ever went through adolescence is the ingrained sociological reaction to not ask questions, just do what the note says and pass it along to the receiving end. Like you have no choice in the matter. The instructions are clear; I must pass this note on or be subjected to the consequences!

I loved Katie for that. I loved that she found hilarity in random acts of frivolity. I loved that she thought of me every Monday, Wednesday, and Friday, at 2:25 p.m. I loved that she would write "the handsome dark-haired man in the front row" and assume everyone would know who that was. And I love that Katie still thinks no matter what other vocation I pursue to support our family, I should never give up on that little writing office with the typewriter that overlooks the ocean.

The Hum of a Dishwasher in Love

Written August 17, 2009

The moment our relationship rounded that final corner and opened up to a full sprint to the Engagement Finish Line, Katie was washing dishes.

I was not.

I was in a play, up on BYU campus. *Ordinary People.*

The play was highly entertaining, but only to those of us in the cast. The other eight folks in the audience gave us a lukewarm reception. Could be that they found dysfunctional families sad or could be that they weren't privy to our myriad of inside jokes that included hidden quotes from other movies, incidental pratfalls, and an RC Cola reference – *during the play.*

I got home that night around 10:30 p.m. and called Katie so she could give me an unbiased opinion on how awesome and funny our play was. (She'd seen it opening night.) This was back in 1995, before email, texting, or even cell phones. So, I had to wait until I got back to my apartment to use a landline to call her – like some sort of barbarian or wild animal!

"Katie?" I asked. "Don't you think it's funny when, at the part in the play when Chris lies to me that I respond, in my best 1920s gangster voice and say, 'Why-I-oughtta…!', even though it takes place in the 80s and we're not gangsters?"

Her response came at lightning speed, and it was difficult to decipher, except I could hear her repeating my name several times. Finally, I was able to make out a "I missed you so much, can you come over right now?!"

Of course, after I literally hung up the phone on the wall, I was on my way. But the funny thing was, I'd just been with her before the play. We hadn't been apart that long. But I hurried anyway because, my goodness, she sounded like she was caught in a gin-raid at a speak-easy!

I kicked the door off the hinges and in slow-motion it fell to the floor of her condo with a thud and a cloud of dust. The moonlight behind me shaped my silhouette and cast a shadow on the clearing haze. The music crescendo-ed. There she stood in the kitchen, her hair blowing from the breeze through the window over the sink, wearing nothing but jeans and a long-sleeve turtleneck under a BYU sweatshirt, with an apron on, plus cleaning gloves and a hairnet. Shoes and socks.

She ran towards me, and I stretched out my arms. She jumped into my embrace.

She was crying. I had no idea why. But we were hugging, and I liked that. Breaking the spell, I asked her what was wrong.

"Nothing," she said. "I'm just so excited to see you, and I love you so much."

I liked where this was going. It seemed things were in my favor, but she was still crying, and I was still confused. Fortunately, she went on.

"I have memories of doing homework late at night on the kitchen table," she started to explain. "My mom would be cleaning the kitchen, and the last thing she would do was start the dishwasher. Once it was running, she would come sit at the table with me. I loved that time. The world had slowed down, she was not multi-tasking, and everything was about our conversation and our relationship. It felt safe. I felt nurtured. I felt loved. And the sound of the dishwasher running has always reminded me of that. Tonight, with nobody else home, I did the dishes, loaded the dishwasher and sat at the kitchen table to do some homework. And as the dishwasher ran, I remembered all those feelings. And I realized that that's how I feel when I'm with you."

As you can imagine, I was thrilled. I was in love and I didn't even care that Katie had distracted me and side-stepped admitting to my face that the play I was in was nowhere near the Coke or Pepsi caliber at all, but was in fact the RC Cola of plays.

A few weeks later, we were engaged.

~

Getting Engaged

Written August 17, 2007

It was the middle of August 1995 when, in one of the most brilliant and intricate sting operations ever pulled off in modern history, I tricked Katie Fillmore into marrying me.

Since that day, she has tricked me a number of times. Her favorite is this thing she does when she's driving the van on a road trip, and she tilts her head so I can't see the left side of her face, and she makes it look like she's totally and completely asleep at the wheel, when in actuality, her left eye is wide open, keeping our family safe from flying off the road into a tree, off a cliff, or into a stranded motorist. I can't say I like this trick, but turnabout's fair play, I suppose.

Like most folks born after 1960, we do in fact have a Wedding Video. And we love to watch it. Sure, the quality is fading, along with my insistence that there is something wrong with the video because my hair was never *that* big, but it is one of the happiest videos you'll ever see. You can't help but smile when you watch it. It was really a great day.

But in addition to our Wedding Video, we happen to have an Engagement Video. Now, this was in an era before everyone and their grandma owned a smart phone and recorded everything they did every day, including their staged engagements. So, it was quite miraculous and serendipitous that we ended up with one at all!

It's not much. But technically, we were never supposed to have one, so that makes it a remarkable, recorded moment. And yes, I am going to tell the story.

It was April 1995. Provo, Utah. The days were a warmish spring, with the nights still quite cool. TLC was warning us not to chase waterfalls and Bryan Adams was demanding to know if we'd ever really – really, really ever loved a woman.

At this point I had known for several months that I wanted to marry Katie. (So yes, Mr. Adams, I believe I have really really loved a woman.) By April, it felt like everything in the universe was coming to a head, with planets aligning – all leading up to a very specific time and place to get engaged.

I knew Katie wanted me to meet her family before we got any more serious. And her family was coming out to Utah for the graduation ceremonies of two of Katie's older sisters, held Thursday, April 27th. Planet 1 aligned.

Katie had torn her ACL in her knee and would be heading back to Kentucky with her family (post-graduation ceremonies) for surgery. They would be leaving the morning of Saturday, April 29th. Planet 2 aligned.

This meant I had a window of Friday, April 28th, to ask Katie to marry me.

Katie's cousin happened to be a jeweler, so I visited him the week prior to Katie's family coming, and I selected The Engagement Ring. He had designed it and he was going to craft it and have it ready for me on Friday morning, so I could propose Friday night. Except that when I called on Thursday to make sure he was ready, he said, "Oh, I messed up on it. I won't have it ready until Monday."

I could tell he was concerned, so I kindly answered back, "Well, Jack-face, if you can't have it ready tomorrow, don't bust your hump to have it ready Monday. She's leaving Saturday." And he responded, "Sorry."

Oh, the humanity! My life was in the toilet. Nothing left to do now but watch Katie leave for Kentucky, unengaged and ready to fall in love with some toothless, shoeless, slack-jawed yokel with an annual crop of Kentucky tobacco big enough to shake a beer keg at. I was depressed.

Friday arrived, and it was a busy day. I was packing to move apartments and Katie was packing to go home for surgery. We didn't see each other much, and the only highlight of the day was that a big group of us friends decided to get together for dinner at The Underground that night. A kind of End of Semester send off before summer, when everyone would be going different directions for a while. A friend of ours, Mike, played guitar at The Underground, and we were all going to hang out, eat, and take a listen.

We were supposed to be meeting in about an hour, and I called Katie to let her know I was going to come pick her up in a bit. I sat on the couch to pack my last box of junk when the phone rang. It was Katie's cousin/my jeweler.

"Hey, your ring is ready."

"Is this some sick joke?"

"It's not a joke. I canceled all my other appointments for the day and finished the ring."

"You're a beautiful man."

"Yes, well, I just left it with Katie's mom, so you can pick it up from her."

"Uhm…you left it with WHO?"

My jeweler didn't know where I lived, or my phone number, but he knew where Katie's mom was staying, so he contacted her, got my phone number, and left the ring with her. Convenient for him, awkward for me. But I was too excited to care!

With only a few minutes to throw everything together, I ran over to Katie's grandpa's house to find my future mother-in-law and, in exchange for a ring, I explained to her that I was going to ask her daughter to marry me that night. Fortunately for me, my mother-in-law was ecstatic and gushed over the ring with me, securing her place in the Best Mother-In-Law Hall of Fame.

The rest of this story is told in fast-framed, *Keystone Cops* fashion.

I ran back to my apartment and handed the ring to my friend, Lincoln. In one long sentence I explained to him that I was going to propose to Katie at The Underground, during our little Have a Great Summer party, that I needed him to go buy roses for Katie and hand them off to our good friend Lisa to bring out to Katie right after I propose, that I needed him to talk to Mike about playing U2's "All I Want Is You" while I propose, and that at some point, after I arrived, I needed him to slip the ring back to me when Katie wasn't looking. He was completely on board and very excited for me.

Then, in maintaining cartoonish, frantic energy, we ran into each other three times and then ran to our different destinations. Me, to pick up Katie, and Lincoln, to The Underground to set everything up.

When I ran into Katie's apartment to pick her up, I realized I needed to CALM DOWN. But it was too late. She came down the stairs, gave me a hug, then stepped back and said, "What's going on? You're shaking."

"Oh. Huh. Must be the heroin."

"Oh, YOU (small chuckle)."

I covered that one pretty well.

We got in the car and I took the longest route possible to get to The Underground. I actually stopped at the video store on the way. *Forrest Gump* had just been released on video that week. And at that moment, my life really was like a box of chocolates. It spoke to me.

Having stalled as long as I could, we finally made our way over to the restaurant. I could only hope that Lincoln had set everything up, and as soon as we walked through the doors I knew everything was in place. I knew this because two of our friends who were supposed to be there that night but who also worked there, Lisa and Rebecca, had just gotten off their shifts, and came running over to us. I mean, they hurdled tables and pushed paying customers out of the way to get to us, so excited were they.

They stopped right in front of us and then Lisa, with her eyes wide open, started talking like the speed-talking Fed Ex Guy. "Yeah, we-just-got-off-our-shifts-but-we're-going-to-stick-around, maybe-get-something-to-eat. Even-Chris-is-coming-over, you-know, just-to-casually-hang-out-and-stuff."

There was this wall of energy coming from the two of them and the hairs on my neck were standing straight up. I was hoping this was all coming across to Katie as casual as Lisa and Rebecca were trying to sell it. Somehow, Katie didn't pick up on it. Not even when Lisa squeezed my hand and looked at me out of the side of her eye. If I didn't propose to Katie soon, it was clear Lisa was going to do it for me.

I couldn't even order anything to eat. My stomach was in knots. We had talked about marriage before, but I still felt like I was taking an anxiety bath. I suppose it's because that is the moment when you say, "Yes, I will spend the rest of eternity with *you*." Plus, we were doing this in front of our friends and strangers.

We sat at the center table, right in front of where Mike was playing. Our good friends Chris and Lisa, who had gotten engaged less than two months before, sat right across from us, and so did our friend Rebecca. Many of our other friends, including my co-conspirator, Lincoln, were also there.

Lincoln and I managed to slip away for a private conversation (no, not in the men's room). He handed over the ring and told me that as soon as I signaled him, he would signal Mike, and Mike would start playing U2's "All I Want Is You." He was going to stop in the middle of the song, Lisa would slip out to bring the roses, and I would drop to my knee and wet my pants.

I sat back down at the table and noticed the faces of several friends surrounding me. Some of them seemed more nervous than me. After what felt like a week, I signaled Linc, and he signaled Mike. Mike started playing. Then, in the middle of the song, he stopped. Then I stood up and announced to the restaurant that I needed everyone's attention to the center of the room. I knelt down and helped Katie stand up (she was still on crutches from tearing the ligament in her knee), and I actually said the words, "Katie, will you marry me?" She said yes – actually she screamed "Yes!" and then started crying. And it was really a very incredible, surreal moment....

And it's captured, forever, on video. Mike, the guitar player, actually had his mom visiting. And she was so proud of her beatnik son, she actually brought a video camera to record him singing.

Out of coincidence, we were getting engaged that night, and there she was to film it. Well, not all of it. She actually only swings the camera around enough to record some very key moments. But now they are immortalized. It wasn't until the next day, when Katie had left with her family for her surgery and I was at dinner with Lincoln and Mike that Mike said, "If you want a copy of that video, just let me know."

"What video?"

"My mom recorded you guys getting engaged last night."

Completely surprised, and quite grateful, I said, "Well frankly, it wasn't any of her business, but if you've got the video..."

UNDERDRESSED FOR THE OCCASION

"Naked people have little or no influence on society."

– Mark Twain

~

Underdressed for the Occasion

Written October 24, 2012

D o you have moments in your family history that probably shouldn't be recorded, much less publicly shared? Perhaps an incident that was neither acknowledged in the moment it happened, nor has it ever been discussed since?

Me neither.

Well, all right. I have one.

It was the summer of 2005. Katie's side of the family was having a Family Reunion at a ranch in southern Utah. A few days prior to the official reunion, many out-of-staters were flying into Las Vegas to stay with us for a day or so, and then driving from there up to the ranch. We thought this was great, as it allowed us some extra time with a handful of siblings and cousins.

It was a Sunday morning and you could hear the mayhem of a full house outside our bedroom doors. We had crammed several families into our home, many with small children, and we were all trying to get ready for church at the same time.

Katie was in front of the mirror in the master bathroom, blow-drying her hair, as I stepped out of the shower. Now, if you must know, we are pretty casual with our nakedness; and additionally, if you must know (you are so nosy!), sometimes I … well, I air-dry. There. I said it.

I suddenly realized that all my bathroom stuff (deodorant, hair gel, toothpaste, smell-good) was still in my racquetball bag from the day before. And my racquetball bag was not in the bathroom. Nope. It was on the bedroom floor, in front of the door. I strutted across the room and had my head buried in my bag as I pulled my stuff out of it … When abruptly, somebody knocked hard and deliberately on the door. THUD, THUD, THUD. (At least, that's how it sounded to my naked ears.)

I tipped my head up and locked eyes with the doorknob. We were nose to nose. My heart stopped, my world went silent, and time froze. A single water drop from my hair ran down my face.

At this point, my brain told me I had two options. Option 1: Frantically yell, "DON'T COME IN!" Or Option 2: Remain silent and wait for them to go away. I went with Option 2 because I was confident that yelling "DON'T COME IN!" would immediately conjure up the image in this poor soul's head of one Ken Craig standing less than three feet away, stark raving naked. And that image isn't doing anybody any favors.

I chose wrong.

Promptly, the doorknob gave, and the door swung open!

As I saw it, at this point, I still had some options. 1. Push the door closed on their face. 2. Pull my bag off the floor and strategically place it like "so" (I'm showing you with my hands right now), or even 3. Jump behind the door!

But no. I chose Option 4: Jump into the open from where you're standing and spread your body as wide as possible as you sail across the room. Yes, jump like you are taking a bullet for the President of the United States, and that bullet simply must not pass by you; naked or not.

It probably looked more like the shot above; though in my mind, it was more like the photo below.

I closed my eyes as I leapt through clear and present danger, because I knew for sure that if this person and I made eye contact, our lives would forever be changed.

And before I landed, I heard a woman's voice yell, "EEEEEEEEEK!" and the door slam.

I ran into the bathroom where Katie was still blow-drying her hair. "Your sister just saw me naked!" I reported, as if I was tattling on her.

"What?" answered Katie, with her head still under a blow-dryer.

"Your sister! She just saw me naked!"

"When?" she responded so calmly.

"Just NOW! A few seconds ago."

"Oh ... I'm sure she didn't mind."

??????????????????????????????

(This is where my brain just fell right out of the back of my head.)

"I DON'T EVEN KNOW WHAT THAT MEANS! SHE "DIDN'T MIND?!" WHAT ARE YOU SAYING TO ME?!

"Just ... I don't know ... you play racquetball ... you're fit ... I'm sure she didn't mind."

"I ... (pointing wildly at my chest) ... I MIND!"

"Were you walking around like that?"

"Yes, in our room!"

"She just walked in?"

"Well, she knocked first, but then walked in."

"She just barged in without waiting for a response?"

"No; I didn't respond, because if I'd yelled not to come in then she would have imagined me naked!"

"Well, she doesn't have to imagine it anymore."

"Who walks into a bedroom when the door is closed?! This is not my fault!"

"Isn't it?! She knocked! You don't have to yell in a panicked voice! You can calmly respond, 'Just a minute' or 'One second.'"

"Oh. Huh. Those both sound pretty great, actually. WHERE WERE YOU 20 SECONDS AGO!?"

I got dressed and finally, after reassuring myself that this would go away and there wasn't really any reason to discuss it further, I headed downstairs. On the way down I thought to myself, "Maybe it wasn't Katie's sister that saw me after all. Maybe it was her cousin…"

For some completely irrational reason, I just knew I would feel better if it had been her cousin. I have absolutely no idea why. We were all similar ages, from similar backgrounds, and followed similar social norms of not being naked in public.

But I sensed that if it had been her cousin, the two of us would be able to just laugh it off quicker. So, I did what any normal individual in my situation would do.

I located Katie's cousin in the living room, walked right up to her, and in a normal voice, just normally said, "Meredith, please tell me that you just saw me naked in my bedroom."

She stared right back into my eyes with a widening smile, not even flinching, and said, "Nope."

"Shoot," I said back.

Well, I had successfully deduced who it was, and now, Meredith probably had, too. We agreed to never discuss it again. And I never brought it up with Katie's sister either. And if she is reading this, please note, there is still no need to discuss anything. I'm fine. You're fine. And I don't keep my bathroom things in my racquetball bag anymore. Now let's all just get back to work. As you were.

Public Service Announcement

Written November 18, 2006

A s the holidays approach and many of you prepare to load up the family car and make the migration back to … well, wherever it is you don't currently live, I would like to take this opportunity to present a Public Service Announcement, brought to you by the makers of Craig Children, and other fine products.

Throughout the course of my life, ladies and gentlemen, I have made more road trips than the Rolling Stones (but without the liquor and with only a fraction of the heroin). And inevitably, during every trip, I have reached that late-night breaking point where my eyes are just not going to stay open any longer. And I know I am not alone in this.

To combat this phenomenon, I have tried the following measures, to no avail:

1. Loud music. I have found this method ineffective, no matter how loud the music. Somehow, even the raucous melodies of Def Leppard become a soft lullaby. Mr. Sandman may start out pouring sugar on me, but soon enough, he is simply pouring sleepy dust in my eyes.

2. Food. Many are the late-night journeys where I have combined my fuel stops with a quick dash into the convenience store to grab an armful of sugary, life-saving goodness. Sodas, M&Ms, Hostess, what have you. I gobble it in record time and enjoy about 10 minutes of alertness. About enough time to get back on the highway. Then I'm not only fighting off sleepiness, but a sugar coma.

3. Face out the window. This is where you roll down the window and stick your face out into the frozen night air – while simultaneously waking up everyone in the car with an oppressive blast of arctic wind. This wakes you up all right, and then the window closes, you shudder once or twice, the heater picks up, and 1.5 seconds later, you're right back where you started.

It was during one of my many road trips during college that I discovered what worked for me, personally. I remember getting drowsy and thinking to myself, "What might keep me awake and alert?" And it dawned on me that being focused on something would help. And while I was too tired to focus on anything profound or life-altering, I knew if I could find something simple that required my attention … some small task … it would keep me alert. So, I undressed.

In a slow and calculated manner, I removed article by article of clothing until I was completely naked. There I was driving 80 mph down the freeway completely in the buff. And then I got dressed again – slowly and calculated, item by item. Small, simple tasks.

Genius? Oh, I don't know. Sometimes these things just come to me. But maybe it is. Maybe it's inspiration. And I'll tell you this – nude driving will keep you awake, if for no other reason, because you now have incorporated the fear of being pulled over by a highway patrol officer or worse yet, crashing and being found naked and unconscious for all the world to see.

I remember the first road trip Katie and I took after we were married. We were driving from Utah to Los Angeles, to interview for an internship with NBC. We got a bit of a late start, and somewhere between Cedar City and St. George it was 1 a.m., and I was getting awfully sleepy. Katie was in the passenger seat, well into a nap, so I had nobody to talk to.

Well, no worries. I was well versed in Plan N.A.K.E.D at this point (**N**ude **A**lert **K**en **E**ffectively **D**riving), so I began the undressing process. I thought nothing of it until my newlywed wife woke up to find a fully nude husband driving 80 mph down I-15, humming "Pour Some Sugar on Me." It occurred to me at this point that prior to our getting married, I had never had the Plan N.A.K.E.D. talk with Katie.

It was a bit of an awkward moment, and I was really starting to wish I hadn't picked up that hitchhiker in Paragonah. (HA! Thank you I'll be here all week!) Katie had an inquisitive look on her face that I had never seen before, nor since. But she just sat up and said, "Is it hot in here or is it just me?"

Nowadays, with five kids traveling with us, I'll admit that my once flawless plan seems unsuitable, and would likely frighten our poor chil-dren. I am now urgently seeking a different method of staying awake. I haven't come up with anything yet, so we will be staying in Las Vegas for the holidays this year, listening to *A Very Merry Def Leppard Christmas* right here in the comfort of our home.

A Soap by Any Other Name

Written August 30, 2005

W e moved into our new home at the end of June, and more ecstatic I could not be. We loved our last home. It was the first home we ever owned. (And by "owned" I mean "owed an obscene amount of money to Washington Mutual.") Two of our children were literally born inside that house, (one on the couch, one on the toilet.), we loved our neighbors, and we loved the low interest rate. But the time had come when we had really outgrown the place. Plus, I didn't want to have to take my daughter into the bathroom one day, point at the toilet, and say, "I'm afraid the rumors are true, Roxanna … this is where we brought you into the world."

As fate would have it, I also started a new job this year. A job that has enabled us to own this new house, no less. (And by "own" I mean "owe an obscene amount of money to IndyMac Bank.") The job is good, the house is wonderful, my family is healthy and happy … but if I'm going to be completely honest, I must admit that my entire sense of accomplishment stems from something else. Soap.

On our first morning in our new home I stepped into the shower to discover a new bar of soap, the likes of which I had never before seen.

"This isn't our standard Spring-scented Ivory," I thought. No, this soap was white…and kind of oval shaped. Hmmm… I picked it up, wetted it in the shower stream, and began rubbing it between my hands to produce a lather – the way God intended.

Sweet saints and soldiers – this soap was fantastic! It smelled of success. It smelled of destiny. It smelled of providence. There is no way that a man having showered with this soap could not have concerted power over his own fate and the fate of the people around him. No sir. This was clandestine soap.

This was the soap of corporate executives. Of media moguls. Of members of the Academy of Motion Picture Arts & Sciences, for crying out loud! This soap had a new convert, to be sure. I became addicted.

My confidence at work – unmatched. My social calendar – filled. My drollness around strangers – above reproach. I was certain that life could never get any better for me, now that I had discovered this life-shifting soap! Psychiatrists should prescribe this stuff, I thought. How much better the world could be if we could all ascertain the power of this soap. Bless you, Katie, my darling bride … bless you for experimenting with new soap.

And then one day the soap had gotten quite small.

"Honey," I shouted from inside the shower, feeling powerful and masculine. "Can you hand me another bar of soap, this one is almost gone."

"Really? Are you using the Ivory?"

"No. That is substandard soap."

"What have you been using?"

"The other soap. The white, oval-shaped soap."

"Oh. Huh. That soap was here *when we moved in.*"

I froze mid-lather, my hands to my face, the stream of water from the showerhead beating against my chest with a deafening reverberation. I was partially horrified that I was using a bar of soap owned and used regularly by a man I had never met, and partially horrified that the soap was almost gone, and I had no idea what it was called or where I could find more of it. I quietly wept, hiding my tears in the shower stream.

The soap is gone now. I guess it's only a matter of time before I can kiss my job and this house goodbye as well. (Who's going to employ a guy that smells like Irish Spring? Well, I don't want to work for that employer, mister. I can't go back to being that guy.)

DEATH STOPPED BY TO SAY HELLO

"I am ready to meet my Maker. Whether my Maker is prepared for the great ordeal of meeting me is another matter."

– Winston Churchill

~

And for My Final Act, Ladies and Gentlemen...

Written October 31, 2006

In all of my 35 years on this planet, my closest brush with death came this past Saturday. Fact is, I hope it never gets any closer than that.

My friend Micah (names have not been changed) owns a couple of what the people in the biz refer to as "quads" and invited me to go riding last Saturday morning. I had ridden a quad one other time in my life, and that was for exactly three minutes, at exactly five miles per hour, with exactly one of my children riding with me. So, when Micah asked me if I had been riding before, my immediate response was, "Of course, dude, what do I look like, some weenus?"

Micah picked me up around 7:00 a.m. and we drove up to Cold Creek, a site up the eastern side of Mount Charleston. We parked his Durango and unloaded the quads from the trailer. Micah had a map of the mountain and some ideas of some pretty amazing areas to see. And truly, the mountain was fantastic – fall colors everywhere and not another living soul.

The air was crisp, and we had dressed for it. I had on several layers of clothing, gloves, a helmet, and eye goggles. In five hours' time we had traversed about 18 miles and covered some pretty beautiful, if not treacherous terrain. Micah was no doubt duly impressed not only by my natural quad-ing skills, but also with my fearless nature and rugged autumn jacket.

Less than half a mile from the peak of the mountain, we ran into a dead-end and decided to turn around and head back. The road we were on was gravelly rather than rocky, and flat enough for us to pick up some speed.

I was trailing Micah and clipping along at about 40 mph when I came around corner into a cloud of dust and some compromised visibility. I should have slowed down, but figured I had accurate enough bearings to know I was fine. That's when my vision cleared to see a 20-foot ravine directly in front of me.

I immediately applied the brake and turned the quad away from the ravine, but with the speed and the sudden turn, I could feel the quad tipping and getting ready to flip. Everything slowed down in my mind and the final thought that ran through my head was, "This is *it*. You have control of nothing and you are going into the ravine."

I don't know how long I was unconscious, but when I came to, I couldn't focus or hold a coherent thought in my head. My mind and my vision were both hazy and I felt like each time I tried to focus my brain would flip over, like it was unsuccessfully trying to balance itself. I wasn't sure where I was or what exactly had just happened. I started to look around and noticed the quad about ten feet from me, sitting upright. I was lying near the bank of the ravine but hadn't gone over the edge. At this point I figured that I had just fallen off, and perhaps nothing too bad had happened.

I started to push my body off the ground and felt a sharp pain across my upper back between my shoulder blades and up through my neck. The left side of my body was in complete agony. I lay back down. I propped my head to look in the other direction. I don't know if my helmet had been knocked off or if I took it off, but it wasn't on anymore. I looked into the road and saw some rather large pieces of the quad spread all over the place. It occurred to me at that point that the quad had flipped at least once, if not more, and just happened to land upright.

I didn't feel I could stand without toppling over, so I pulled myself up on the quad and hunched over it. The only image I could spotlight for any length of time was my family. I kept seeing Katie's face and the faces of my cute children. And there was kind of this non-verbal motivation to be okay, so I could be with them again. But that was it. No other images came into my mind; nothing else motivated me to do anything.

I knew Micah would eventually notice that I wasn't behind him, then stop and wait for me, and when I didn't come, he would come back. I don't know how much time had passed, but soon I could hear his quad coming up the hill.

I don't recall much of our reunion, (or the next couple of hours), but I know that Micah kept trying to keep me mentally engaged. My answers were short.

"Are you okay?"

"I don't know..."

"What happened?"

"I can't really remember."

"Should Harrison Ford really be making a fourth Indiana Jones movie?"

"I … can't decide."

We were miles from anybody, I wasn't dead, and our only plan was to get safely down the mountain. I climbed on the back of Micah's quad and he started down. We were so far over the mountain from where we started that we were actually closer to Pahrump than Las Vegas. (Pahrump's Motto: Land Of 1,000 *X-Files* Episodes.)

We rode about six miles when we happened upon a couple of guys unloading some quads from their trailer. Well, one was unloading the quads, the other toothless fellow was playing "Dueling Banjos" on his own banjo and telling Micah he had a pretty smile.

Actually, body piercing aside, these were some very nice folks who didn't hesitate for a second to load their quads back up and drive us twelve miles into Pahrump. I don't recall the trip down much, except that it was bumpier than I would have liked. I was having difficulty holding my head up and my breathing felt labored. I didn't think my neck was broken, but it felt so vulnerable, the paranoid part of me was sure that all I had to do was turn my head wrong and I would be doing special tours at our nations' high schools, talking from my wheelchair about how to have a positive attitude in the face of adversity.

They dropped us off at the Pahrump hospital. It was a Saturday, and it was Pahrump, so I'm sure they had their best veterinarian on hand to check me out. They put a neck brace on me, sat me in a wheelchair, and wheeled me back for some x-rays. I was in and out of consciousness through it all, and I'm glad, because the parts where I was awake were extremely painful. The x-rays showed no broken bones, much to my relief. So, the vet wrote me out a prescription for Lortab and recommended I take it with two helpings of Alpo, for healthy teeth and a shinier coat.

Micah had called our friend Bob (again, names have not been changed) and asked him to come rescue us from Pahrump-a-pum-pum. Bob's lovely wife joined the Extraction Team and dropped Bob off at Cold Creek to pick up Micah's Durango and trailer. Bob then drove around the mountain to Pahrump, a 40-minute drive if you don't stop at any of the five brothels greeting you at the entrance to Pahrump. (Bob made it in 45, but we gave him the benefit of the doubt.)

We went back up the mountain to retrieve what remained of the quad I was driving. I waited in the car, but Micah and Bob put on their CSI baseball caps and started singing songs from The Who as they examined the crime scene with flashlights in daylight.

Micah wondered aloud how I didn't, logistically, go into the ravine. And Bob commented that he had never seen anyone simply walk away from an accident that damaged a quad so severely. At first, I thought they were complimenting me on my deft ability to remain calm under intense pressure and my instinctual stuntman reflexes. Then I realized they were saying that there had to have been some divine intervention and that I was very fortunate to only be severely banged up.

After a long drive, Micah and Bob, my personal heroes, dropped me off at home and I immediately called dibs on our couch. Katie went out to pick up my Lortab and I actually put some finishing touches on a talk I was supposed to deliver at church the next day.

I took the Lortab and went to bed, but then woke up at 3 a.m. to throw said Lortab right up and out of my already aching body. I tried Motrin, and it seemed to be milder on my stomach.

Yesterday I left the house long enough to go the doctor, and the good doctor said I have a concussion and that it will probably take 4 to 8 weeks for me to completely mend. There is some extensive bruising and swelling up the left side of my body, but because of how much clothing I was wearing, the only significant loss of skin was on my left forearm, and one slash across my hip. I'll be on the couch for the next couple of days, but I know the day is coming when I will physically be able to do whatever I want once again.

You don't walk away from something like this without learning something, and I certainly have. I am still here because I have something to accomplish. Could be supporting my wife, could be raising my children, could be attending the opening night of *Raiders of the Lost Ark IV*. Some mysteries of life you never really figure out. But it's nice that I still have some time to give it a shot.

Corporate Challenge

Written April 30, 2009

In Las Vegas, the best thing to happen to the business world is – hands-down – our local Corporate Challenge. What's this you say? You've never heard of this legendary social and physical cocktail of the business world? Well, pull up a pommel horse while I tempt your ears with tales of immense competition, tremendous physical feats, and pudgy middle-aged dudes who show up for the Speed Walk race in flip flops and black dress socks.

See friends, each year, for over a quarter of a century now, the folks of the City of Las Vegas have slapped together this thing called Corporate Challenge, wherein local businesses from throughout the valley can fire one of their employees and use his annual salary to pay the inflated entry fee, make some un-wearable team tee-shirts and have the chance to come together in amateur athletic events while making every attempt to not look as pitiful as the competition.

According to their website, Corporate Challenge promotes, enables, and supports teamwork, company pride, and corporate wellness. But more importantly, it gives you the opportunity to see what your boss looks like in shorts. That's great ammo for taking him down a peg. The next time you're up for your annual review and he says he's not sure about your job performance, you just pipe up, "Well I'm not sure about YOUR performance on the soccer field, Mr. Falls-Every-Time-He-Kicks! By the way, were those YOUR legs, or were you riding on top of a chicken?"

Not sure you want to play soccer? Not a problem. It turns out Vegas is not only a morally free-thinking city, but is also quite liberal with their definition of "sports," as well. Corporate Challenge offers 33 different events, including archery, bocce, golf, poker, tennis, swimming, volleyball, buffet eating, binge drinking and pole dancing.

Myself? The only sport I can play with any confidence where I will not embarrass myself is racquetball. And pole dancing, but they don't allow men to compete. Discriminating fatheads. However, the night racquetball was on the docket, I had a previous commitment. No racquetball for me. I was devastated. Rumor is I could have taken the whole thing. That rumor may or may not have been started by me.

Feeling that I'd let my company down, I signed up to participate in events that were not necessarily my forte, but that needed somebody with both a pulse and the ability to talk trash to the competition. I assumed that even though I didn't run, I could still compete, figuring that my regular regimen of racquetball playing must keep me in decent aerobic shape. Plus, in the spirit of humility, I will tell you that I have strong legs and a bum that could crack walnuts.

My first event was the 5K. Despite having two parents who have been runners their whole lives, I did not receive that insanity gene. I loathe running. Unless a bear is chasing me, or Billy Ray Cyrus is about to take the stage, I'm just not going to turn and start running. No iPod mix or crowd cheering is going to motivate me either. My mom used to explain why she loved it. "It's great exercise." "It suppresses your appetite and you lose weight." "It's when I have time to myself and I can say my prayers."

Finally, something we agreed on. Because when I run, I'm also praying. But my prayers usually go something like, "Please, for the love of heaven, don't let me die out here! (pant, pant) Where am I? Please stop my heart from trying to shoot out of my chest like an alien. (pant, pant) Please, don't let anybody I know drive by and see me face-down, drinking out of the gutter and grateful to do so."

Yet, surprisingly, in the 5K, I came in fifth in my age bracket (which must have been ages 35 to 82).

Two days later was Track & Field. I have never run track, but I agreed to, because they needed somebody to run the 400-meter. I was fine with running the 400-meter. In fact, my only objection was to running hurdles. Those scare me. There must be 1001 ways to maim yourself on a hurdle, and most of them involve your groin.

The competition started at 6 p.m., but with so many events, coupled with poor organization by the Corporate Challenge folks, I didn't run until 9:30 p.m. And I hadn't eaten since my delicious burrito at lunch. I tried to do some prep work beforehand and asked around about this enigma of the track and field events: The 400. Some people told me it was a sprint. Then others said it wasn't. Then others asked why in the world I was running the 400, and they kind of wringed their hands together and cackled at my not-knowing anything about it. This made me nervous. Then somebody told me the 400 was an entire lap around the track. Then everybody else confirmed that. Then I wet my pants. It didn't help that my lovely wife and our six adorable children were all in the stands, watching and assuming that I would do wonderfully.

The air felt heavy, like it had eaten a big meal. I felt a knot in my stom-ach. I wasn't sure what to expect, how to pace myself, and when to start praying. Then I got my smarts on and decided I would just pace myself based on the guy directly in front of me.

At that point, fate stepped in and openly mocked me. I took my place on the track and found that we were starting in a staggered position. Fanned out. I was on the outer most lane, meaning that I started most forward. Meaning that there was nobody in front of me against whom to pace myself. Who could have seen that coming?

The gentleman shot the firing gun, and I took off. I mean I ran like a bear was chasing me and Billy Ray was saddled on his back singing "Achy Breaky Heart." I didn't look behind me. I didn't look to the side. I didn't look up. Silence fell around me, and all I could hear were my lungs. And man, were they ticked! They were yelling all kinds of pro-fanity at me, including some Swahili words I didn't recognize. I kept sprinting, figuring if I slowed at all, I was never going to pick back up. Now my legs were pitching a fit. They were threatening to go on strike, and they knew the lungs would join them immediately. I continued to sprint. Now my stomach was about to show who was boss. "Don't make me search for that burrito," it said, "I'll find it, and I'll embarrass you right here at the 300-mark. Don't think I won't. I wasn't particularly happy to have it here in the first place."

I kept sprinting. Only now, it didn't feel like sprinting. It felt like that bear was going to catch me. My whole body was shutting down. Then, I was pretty confident I could taste blood in my mouth. But what scared me worse was that I was pretty sure it was blood coming from my bleeding eyeballs. Then, right at the end, I saw the guy in the lane next to me pass me. And then the guy next to him. And then, permanently disfigured by the 400, I crossed the finish line.

Third Place.

Some coworkers were there to congratulate and cheer, but it was hard to see them, because I was rapidly losing my vision. Walking like an inebriate, drunk on his own blood, I strolled over to my family, not in a hurry to get there and have one of my children demand to be carried to the van.

I sat in the van, having to consciously force air in and out of my body, or die. And I must admit, I would have been fine either way. No more running for me. Ever. I will be proud to be the dinner for a hungry bear.

I did participate in one other Corporate Challenge event. A few days after running the 400-meter, I took a position on our company's Sand Volleyball team. Remember the volleyball scene in *Top Gun*? We looked nothing like that. For one thing, none of us were Scientologists. For another, Kenny Loggins had not agreed to provide us with a theme song. Billy Ray probably would, but we ain't askin'.

With an Eye on the Future

Written March 24, 2007

Apart from my insistence that there be at least one carton of ice cream in the freezer at all times, I don't ever really take the occasion to spoil myself. Not even in the world of technology, which is perpetually producing gadgets in which I am most intrigued. Alas, I don't own an iPod, a plasma TV, or a cell phone that takes pictures, browses the Internet, or performs lipo after a heavy meal. But this year, for my birthday, I spoiled myself.

About a year ago I decided to start putting aside some money for laser eye surgery. I am slightly nearsighted, and my vision isn't so awful that I need to constantly wear glasses, but it is bad enough that I need to always have them with me, just in case somebody says, "Hey, that guy 15 to 20 feet in front of you is pointing a gun at you," thus, giving me time to take my glasses out of my pocket and observe said gun-toting man. Imagine my embarrassment if I never noticed and actually walked into the guy! (You can see already my dire need for laser eye surgery. It was becoming a matter of life and death, people!)

I had seen many promotional ads throughout the valley for laser eye surgery, with prices ranging from the thousands to one place that offered a free Justin Timberlake CD with each surgery. ("Help Justin bring sexy back, with a new pair of eyes!") I finally decided on one particular eye surgery center, and it was my surgery center of choice for one simple reason: They seemed like they were from the future. So advanced were they, their slogan genuinely read, "Where tomorrow's technology is here today!"

When I walked into the fancy waiting room, I felt like I was in the future. (Like, 2010, at least.) (And you won't believe this, but *The View* is still on in 2010, playing on waiting room televisions all across the nation.) The décor was futuristic, and even their speech seemed slightly futuristic. I was expecting a robot to bring me some sort of mango-colored liquid refreshment as I sat in the waiting room perusing an eye surgery menu that included such options as x-ray vision and digital zoom, all while watching a still-very-angry Rosie O'Donnell.

After a consultation where they ran several tests to determine if I was a "good candidate" for laser eye surgery ("good candidate" = "willing to pay"), we set up an appointment for the procedure. And that procedure took place last Wednesday afternoon.

The Lasik center makes it perfectly clear that you need to bring somebody else with you to the procedure, as you will not be able to drive yourself home. So, I went by the house to pick up Katie and say goodbye to the kids. I have never had surgery of any kind, and although this was supposed to be no big whoop, as far as surgery goes, my mind started to wonder.

Katie asked me to read a book to Roxanna and lay her down for her nap before we left, and as I started to walk out of the bedroom, I turned to look at her. She has the bluest eyes and the cutest smile, and she happened to have her hair up in what I affectionately refer to as a "big girl bun." And suddenly, uninvited, the thought actually crossed my mind, "What if this is the last time you see your daughter's face? What if things go horribly wrong and you completely lose your vision? What if the last book you ever read in this lifetime is *Pirates Don't Change Diapers*?"

I felt a little pierce of panic as I kissed the other kids goodbye and told them we'd be right back. I don't know if it's okay to pray over elective surgery ("…and please bless me in my vanity that my non-obligatory surgery will go well. Amen"), but I did anyway.

We arrived at the center and I was taken back to the prep room. This is where they medicate you so you are completely relaxed and enjoy a pain-free procedure. Now, keep in mind that I don't even take aspirin for headaches, so I my tolerance level for medication is pretty low. It doesn't take much. Nevertheless, they gave me 5 mg of a sedative called Diazepam, and two tablets of Xanax. (Xanax slogan: Have a nice ride!)

They took me to the procedure room and had me climb up on the table. I could see Katie outside the room, looking through the observatory glass. And that's about the last coherent memory I have of that day. The rest is somewhat sketchy.

I do remember the laser machine being pulled over my face, and the restraints that pulled my eyes open and held them in place. It was uncomfortable, but not at all painful. Apparently, they then had me go into another room and did some more work, then took me into another, dark room, where they had Katie come in and they reviewed all the different drops I should be using over the next week to keep my eyes infection-free and well lubricated. I say "apparently" because I remember none of this.

I recall the doctor's assistant who walked me out to the car. I remember I was just alert enough to wonder to myself, "Who does this guy think he is, helping me out to the car? I'm fine." But clearly, I was not. I don't remember getting in the car, I don't remember the drive home, I don't remember Katie going into Walgreens to fill one of my eye-drop prescriptions, I don't remember getting out of the car and walking into the house.

Katie was taking the kids to a birthday party, so she was trying to get me set up on the couch before leaving. I do remember her helping me out of my clothes and into my pajamas in the most unromantic way. We were in the kitchen, I think, and I had the nerdiest protective goggles taped to my face. I grabbed some chips and juice and meandered to the couch. Before Katie left I asked her to turn the TV on so I could just listen to it (since I couldn't watch anything yet). She humored me and turned it on as she left, but I don't recall one, single line of dialogue. I don't remember eating any chips either, but according to Katie and the vacuum, when she got home, I had unsuccessfully attempted to eat a number of them.

I didn't wake up until the next morning. And since then, I have been putting about 23 different drops in my eyes on about 18 different cycles. I feel like I am crying all the time. But other than fighting dryness, my eyes are not in any pain. They say it takes 4 to 6 weeks to completely heal and adjust and already I've noticed a difference in my sight. Still, there are times when things are clear and there are times when things are hazy, and at night, I see these halos around everything. It's like I'm in some 1970's R&B video. They say all of this is normal and part of the healing phase. And I believe them. After all, they already know I'll be fine. They're from the future.

The Case of the Unresolved Footsteps

Written October 25, 2005

The year was 1995. Katie and I were married that August and were living in Provo, Utah that fall, where we attended BYU. To help with rent and to help Katie's family, we lived in the basement apartment of Katie's grandfather's house. It was a yellow, two-story house on 50 East, right behind the Brick Oven, if you're familiar with that Italian eatery. Rather capacious for the location, and quite outdated in comparison to the new student apartments across the street, it looked out of place.

Katie's grandfather had experienced a number of strokes in his old age and was not the picture of health. He could barely move on his own and required others to help him bathe, eat, and change his clothes. He didn't need any help going to the bathroom, however, because he did that wherever and whenever he pleased.

Though the bedrooms were on the second story, to help Grandpa get around, he and his sleeping arrangements had been moved to the main floor. The four bedrooms upstairs were spacious, along with a full bathroom and several sizable closets that were used for either storage or just left empty. With nobody living up there, and no maids, the upstairs was always very still and dusty. It was like nobody had been up there since 1857, when the Saints built the first two-story house in Provo.

Sometimes, when I was the only one home (besides Grandpa), I liked to go upstairs and pretend I ran an old museum. I would give tours and explain how the rooms were used to house all 18 of George Soderborg's children, and how the oldest children would actually select one of the roomy closets as their bedroom, just for the sake of having some privacy! (Then I'd chuckle to myself, assuming the folks taking the tour would equally be amused at my witty monologue that juxtaposed the children of centuries past with the children of today, and how they really aren't that different after all.)

The main floor featured the front room, where Grandpa spent most of his time watching television and spitting out his pills that we had given him about 10 minutes earlier, with a dining room and a kitchen behind the front room. Off to the side was a parlor that had been turned into Grandpa's bedroom. And our basement apartment was directly under his bedroom. There was a set of stairs that went up from the back of our apartment into the kitchen on the main floor, and that was the path we usually traveled to go up and check on Grandpa and take care of him.

One night, in the middle of the night, Grandpa fell out of bed. Turned out he was coherent enough to recognize he had to go to the bathroom and wanted to try and make it on his own, bless him. Unfortunately, he got as far as sitting up in bed…then he sort of just fell out of it and onto the floor. The thud woke me up and I went upstairs, hoisted him up off the floor, checked his diaper, and put him back in bed. I mention this only so you understand how clearly one could hear things going down in Grandpa's room.

We had lived in the apartment just shy of two months when one of the most unsettling things took place one evening, 'round midnight.

Katie and I were going to bed and had most likely just finished chatting about how nobody could possibly ever be in love as much as us, and even though we were newlyweds, we would totally act the same giddy way our whole lives, because we were awesome, and we would always find each other's belches endearing and everything we did would be cute forever and ever. We had been lying there in the dark for just a few minutes – you know those minutes, when it's late, dark, and quiet, and you are juuuust about to doze off, but still about 15% alert. Somewhere between conscious and unconscious. I was almost there, when suddenly, there were five distinct, deliberate, and pounding footsteps running across the floor above us. We both shot up in bed, looked at each other, and shouted "What was THAT?!" I'm telling you, it couldn't have been better choreographed if we were on a movie set.

I physically jumped out of bed. "Did you hear that?!"

"Was that right above us?!" asked a panicked and newlywed-cute Katie.

I understood what she meant – she was saying. "Isn't that Grandpa's room?"

"That couldn't have been Grandpa," I said. "I hoisted him off the floor the other night. He's like an enormous sack of Hogi Yogi. That was something else. *Somebody is in the house.*"

Having almost drifted off for the night and then to be shocked into a state of panic, my adrenaline was already hummin'. I ran up the back stairs, through the kitchen, and into Grandpa's room. He didn't budge. Still snoring, wrapped under his blankets, he was unaware of anything. I did a lap around the main floor – through the front room, the dining room, the kitchen – I saw no signs of anything. My guts imploded, I grabbed the fireplace poker, and I took off up the stairs. I could almost hear the people yelling at my movie screen "Don't go up the stairs!!!!! You'll kill yourself!!!! WHY is he going up the stairs?! Oh, now I HOPE he dies if he's THAT stupid!"

I didn't turn on any lights, for fear of giving away my exact location to the intruder. I ran into every bedroom and closet, ripping the doors open, each time fully expecting to confront somebody. I had never been so hopped up on adrenaline. When I tore open the final door to reveal absolutely nothing, I paused only for a second before the horrible thought came to me, "He's run down the back stairs into my apartment and has Katie!"

Faster than I had run up the stairs, I ran back down, through the kitchen, down another flight of stairs and into my little apartment. There was Katie, sitting up in bed with the covers pulled up to her chin.

"Who is it? Who was there?"

"There's nobody there. There is not one soul in this house beyond us and Grandpa."

I went back up and took a more calculated and leisurely trip through the house, paying more attention to detail and looking to see if there were any small signs of disturbance. I couldn't see a thing.

It was a few months after that, when we were sharing this experience with some of Katie's family that we were told Katie's uncle used to live in that very basement apartment, years before us. Used to. He had moved back home, due to some struggles with emotional and mental imbalances. He had struggled for years with some very real bouts of depression. He killed himself while living in that very apartment.

Don't Believe the Great White Hype

Written March 8, 2007

During this time of great political unrest and in an era where American citizens take offense when no offense is intended, I hesitate to bring up any hot topics. But I will, because if you aren't standing for something, you stand for nothing.

I am vehemently opposed to sharks. Hate them. I looooooathe sharks. I don't have one good thing to say about them. If I were stood before a shark, handed a baseball bat, and told by a judge that if I beat that shark's face in then I would be sentenced to death, I would say, "For my final meal, your honor, I want to eat this very shark." And then I would begin whacking that sucker until it was dead ten times over.

If the above paragraph offends you, you may not want to read any further. You should probably also remove my contact information from your e-database, my family's name from your Christmas card list, and my birthday reminder (March 17th) from your Yahoo Birthday Calendar Reminder thingee. You'll have no need for these things anymore since you are dead to me, you communist, liberal, shark-sympathizer.

I suppose my hatred for these evil predators all started when, as a child, I realized my precious, innocent life would one day end in a violent shark attack. Some people want to blame this on several viewings of *Jaws* before I was nine years old; but I implore you – look at the facts. I was neither afraid of dying by the hands of Lex Luthor nor toxic beer, though I watched both *Superman* and *Strange Brew* on multiple occasions.

My morbid fascination with these horrid beasts has pushed me to the limits of watching Discovery Channel's *Shark Week* from under the covers and between my fingers. I am especially appalled by these video segments that try to paint sharks as the victims of the world. PUH-lease. "A shark's worst enemy is actually mankind." Bullsugar. A shark's worse enemy is…a larger shark! I'm not even a marine biologist, and I'm calling that one.

Have you seen the segments where they have these local tour guides in South Africa actually lean out of the boat and pet the stomachs of Great Whites that come up to the boat? *Pet their stomachs!* This kind of propaganda is worse than any snuff film. I mean, to actually encourage people to pet a Great White! "The most misunderstood animal," indeed. People, wake up! That shark is no dummy. It is mugging for the camera, knowing the thousands of Midwesterners watching will think, "Jeepers, I had them all wrong. Honey, pack a lunch. We're heading to the coast to pet a Great White." Honestly, do you want the terrorist to win? (And by "terrorists," I mean "sharks.") Stay away from sharks, folks; and for that matter, stay away from South Africans that pet them. I think they may be getting kickbacks or something.

If you want to know how sharks really behave, rent the documentaries *Deep Blue Sea* (starring Samuel L. Jackson and LL Cool J – also not fans of South Africa), and *Jaws IV: This Time It's Personal*. These are true stories, documenting that sharks have personal vendettas against humans. And they will hunt us down, if we do not act first. Don't consider this a political agenda. Consider it a call to arms!

WHEN THINGS GO SIDEWAYS

"Don't you quit. You keep walking. You keep trying. There is help and happiness ahead. Some blessings come soon, some come late, and some don't come until heaven; but for those who embrace the gospel of Jesus Christ, they come. It will be all right in the end. Trust God and believe in good things to come."

— Jeffrey R. Holland

Unexpected Plans

Written May 22, 2010

Last week Katie was three months pregnant for the seventh time. This week she's not.

It didn't sneak up on us, but I'm not sure how you prepare for something like that. Katie knew something had been wrong for a few days and was grappling with the possibility of a miscarriage long before I considered it. And even though she told me when her concern started, I dismissed it. I didn't discount that something might be wrong or insist that it wasn't a miscarriage. But I held on to the thought, or maybe hope, that it was something else. Something less definite.

I don't think I realized how much of that day for Katie was spent processing what was most likely happening or what could be happening or what she hoped wasn't happening. As the husband, without the constant reminder that life is growing within me, I operated on the daily assumption that when Katie wasn't telling me something, it meant that everything was fine. And when she did tell me something, I could take a moment to wish and hope it away.

I prayed often for Katie. More than morning and night. But I remember the palpable moment I realized that my prayers and supplications were subconsciously or maybe intuitively always for Katie, and not necessarily the baby. And I think that's when I started to slowly, but not out loud, accept what was already impressing upon me in small waves.

This baby was not coming.

Over the next few days, we didn't discuss it much. I didn't understand what might be happening, so I didn't know what to prepare for. I would often hug her and ask, "Are you okay?"

She would look away, distracted, dealing with her own feelings. "Yes," she said simply, and moved on with her tasks.

It seemed so ineffectual, merely asking if she were 'okay.' I wished I could tell her what was really in my heart. I wanted to say, "I'm so sorry this is happening to you. I'm so sorry I can only stand here completely helpless and watch you emotionally dragged and quartered. I'm sorry I don't know how to make this all go away and heal your body and strengthen your soul. Please tell me what I can do to show my concern. Please tell me that you're not 'okay,' but that if I were to do this or that, you would be. And please, please don't let me go through this by myself."

Then, late one evening, Katie asked me for a priesthood blessing. I knew the request was time-sensitive, so I immediately called a close friend and asked him to come assist me in administering to my wife. As I placed my hands on Katie's head, I could feel how loved she was by her Father in Heaven. How known she was. How important.

I waited for the clarity to come that all would be well with the baby, but it wasn't happening. I waited longer. Never had I struggled more against the impulse to mix my emotions with the revelation I was receiving on somebody's behalf. Everything in me wanted to tell Katie that she would be blessed to give birth to a beautiful baby and her body would heal. Life would be as wonderful as she hoped.

But those impressions never arrived. I found myself making all kinds of additional promises to Father, if only He would grant us this one blessing. But I knew what needed to be said. I felt impressed to promise Katie that this experience would draw her closer to Him; that whether a baby came or not, she would be at peace in her heart and mind, and in her soul. Somehow, that knowledge brought me a degree of hope that I had not anticipated.

The next morning Katie seemed remarkably calm. Not carefree, but peaceful. She said she knew this pregnancy would not develop into a child. And she felt calm and comforted by the blessing. I could see that she was blessed with understanding and insight. I felt reassured by her confidence. My feelings up to that morning had truly been focused on Katie's well-being. A miscarriage would affect her physically, as well as emotionally and mentally. My understanding and acceptance of what was happening were a direct response to hers; I was relieved at her confidence and was now determined that everything would be fine. If Katie was at peace, so was I.

Right?

Wrong.

I left for work that morning, hoping that the background noise of the radio would provide a needed distraction during my commute. I was ten minutes into my drive when the world suddenly slowed down and my mind became singularly focused.

I began to process my own reaction to the reality that a child I was anxious to know and love would not be arriving. I felt like I was going to miss the chance to meet somebody who would have affected my life in a beautiful way … and there was no way to retrieve that specific opportunity. Suddenly, I felt swallowed up in sadness. I wasn't angry or resentful. I didn't feel cheated or that life was unfair. I just felt sad. And that sadness enveloped me.

The radio became so hushed I just turned it off. I became unaware of other cars, other drivers. The air was still and stifling, and I felt energy draining off me like steam. When I arrived at the office, I pulled into the parking lot and sat in my car, no initiative to leave my seat.

My emotions are very near the surface under even the most benign circumstances; so with the profound sadness I was experiencing, I found that I was crying, quietly. I wasn't overwhelmed with emotions, nor did I feel that my exterior was cracking. But I knew that I didn't feel like talking about what was going on.

I worked half the day and then left for an ultrasound appointment with our midwife. As Katie and I drove to the office, our conversation included speculations from one side of the spectrum to the other. From "Maybe I was never pregnant?" to "What if we're completely off and everything is okay?" But when the ultrasound showed what we had already suspected, that a miscarriage was imminent, we weren't startled.

That sadness briefly stung my heart again, and I studied Katie's face, searching for any detectable sorrow. I thought I could see it, but it was buried under a brave, accepting face, so I didn't say a word to her. I felt like speaking would have pulled the foundational block out from under her pyramid of strength, and her calm exterior might have given way. And that just seemed unnecessary. So I simply squeezed her hand.

We drove home somewhat oddly comforted in knowing for certain where we were at, physically. We didn't say anything to anybody else, as we hadn't told anybody yet, not even our parents. The next couple of days were just watching and waiting, but brought us closer. I felt conscious of Katie and what was going on inside her.

At the end of that week, my parents were set to arrive at our house for the weekend, and literally, as I heard my kids squealing that Grandma and Grandpa were here, Katie found me and told me that it had just happened. She cried a light, heartfelt sigh of relief, finally feeling that she had turned a page and felt closure from a long, uncertain experience. I hugged her so close I wasn't sure if my hug was sustaining her or vice versa.

I walked outside and met my parents at the car. I hugged them, helped grab their stuff, and then told them a little about what the last week had been like. I wanted to let them know so they could be sensitive to Katie.

My dad and I were taking my boys camping for the night, and Katie and my mom and the girls had planned to do a Girls' Night at home. As Katie went into the kitchen to start their special dinner, my mom pulled Katie into her and said, "Don't you worry about dinner. We're going out. Let's take it easy tonight."

I watched Katie melt into my mom's embrace, crying. Of course, it was more than the promise that she wouldn't have to cook dinner. It was being understood, being cared for. It was the profound link between women, between mothers. It was an answer to prayer and the fulfillment of a blessing. My mom had had a miscarriage between my two youngest brothers and so understood much more deeply than I, though

I wanted to. And Katie felt that. I will always be grateful that my mom was there; that she is exactly who she is, with the instincts that she has, and the love she's had for Katie since day one.

As I thought about that moment I realized how many people I know and love who have had miscarriages. But for how common they are, rarely are they discussed. I imagine it's because the event may be common, but the experience is personal. It was for us. It seems like a very private grieving; mourning the loss of possibilities, of plans.

I'll always remember the touch of sadness that accompanied this unique experience of 'what might have been.' But through it all, I've known Heavenly Father is mindful of us, that He's been aware of our anxiety, our sorrow. And I know He is aware of our unwavering gratitude for the blessing of family.

'Children are an heritage of the Lord,' the Psalmist writes. I couldn't agree more.

The Slump

Written March 4, 2013

Five months ago I moved my family from Las Vegas, Nevada to Orem, Utah. There were several reasons we did this. Some of those reasons were super clear to me, and some were not. Some were public, and some were personal. Some I'm still not sure of yet. But the path was illuminated and we felt an internal nudge to walk that path. So we did.

This move included the process of finding a new job. And ... everybody relax ... I finally found The One. In fact, I start today, and I am really, really excited!

If you've never been out of work for longer than two weeks, please allow me to share a just a few personal observations:

1. It is the easiest thing in the world to "feel busy." You will sometimes wonder how you ever found time to have a full-time career and do everything else. Your wife will ask you to go to the grocery store, and your response will be, "WHAT? That's, like, my entire afternoon!" And then when she asks you what you're so busy with…the only thing you'll be

able to think of is that all five seasons of *Alias* are now on Netflix, and those episodes aren't going to watch themselves!

2. Up to now, you have been unable to fully fathom both the glory and hazard that is Netflix Streaming.

3. There will come a day when you are standing in front of the bathroom mirror, and you have the razor in your hand, and the thought will come to you, "Who am I shaving for? Seriously, WHO cares if I'm clean shaven?" And with a smirk on your face, you'll put the razor away. Then you'll be surprised to notice that you're wearing jeans... the same pair of jeans you've been wearing for four days. And they do nothing for your figure. And you'll be disgusted with yourself. So you'll throw those jeans in a dirty clothes pile, and you'll go the entire morning pants-less. There will be whispered concerns between family members, but nobody will actually confront you; because clearly, you have only one marble left rolling around in that noggin of yours.

4. There will be moments where you absolutely do not feel like talking to anyone. Because even when they are genuinely concerned about your well being, you have to give them a lame update. And you start to feel that, in addition to being a disappointment to yourself, now you're letting them down as well.

5. You will appreciate the vulnerability of others like never before.

6. You'll develop a deepened repugnance for Know-It-Alls.

7. You will have conversations with your spouse that will sound vaguely familiar to this conversation from the 1983 movie *Mr. Mom*:

Caroline (Teri Garr): You wanna talk about this shirt Jack?

Jack (Michael Keaton): All right.

Caroline: You've been wearing this shirt around the house for about two weeks now – the shirt could walk around by itself! Why don't you retire that thing to the Dry-Cleaning Hall of Fame?

Jack: Because it's a comfortable shirt.

Caroline: Jack, take a look at yourself; you're really throwing in the towel, honey.

Jack: My brain is like oatmeal. I yelled at Kenny today – for coloring outside the lines! Meagan and I are watching the same TV shows … and I'm liking them! I'm losing it!

Or something like this:

You: I'm sorry.

Spouse: For what?

You: For failing.

Spouse: Failing at what?

You: You name it.

Or maybe even something like this:

You: "The problem is I'm not qualified to do anything."

Spouse: "You are qualified to do everything!"

You: "I've never done anything great."

Spouse: "Everything you do is great!"

You: "Just saying the opposite of what I'm saying doesn't build confidence in me."

Spouse: "So you want me to stop?"

You: "…Not really."

8. You will watch Inspirational Messages clips like "Good Things to Come," the one based on Elder Holland's talk, "An High Priest of Good Things to Come," and you'll wish that in all this "down time" you could have dinner with Elder Holland and have him personally encourage you and tell you, "Don't you quit. You keep walking. You keep trying. There is help and happiness ahead. Some blessings come soon. Some come late. And some don't come until heaven. But for those who embrace the gospel of Jesus Christ…they come. It will be all right in the end. Trust God. And believe in good things to come."

9. People will ask you if you are enjoying some "down time" to do whatever it is you have always wanted to do. Write, sculpt, paint, lose weight, master the art of kung fu, create an app, become a stunt driver, start your midwifery practice…whatever. (They mean well, so don't punch them in the throat.) You have to remember that when you're in the World of the Employed, having "free time" seems like the ultimate gift. But when you are in the World of the Unemployed, that "free time" and "energy to be creative" and "desire to develop new passions" and "need to wear pants" is completely choked out by the daily anxiety that despite no money coming through your door, it continues to fly out your windows.

10. If you are blessed to be married to Katie then you will take profound comfort in her unparalleled level of confidence that all things will work together for your good, that you will be blessed to come off the conqueror and that somehow you have the abilities to provide for your family. And that she will be crazy about you, come what may.

11. You will read scriptures and your Patriarchal Blessing and remember other priesthood blessings and counsel you've received, and you will be reassured and have fresh hope and courage fill your soul. Then it will be after lunch that same day, and your surroundings aren't any different than they've been for days. And you will conclude, "I know that if I am worthy of these blessings then the Lord will make good on all His promises. So...since the Lord cannot lie, and these blessings are eluding me...I must not be worthy of them. What am I doing wrong?" And so you'll take it to the Lord over and over, and ask Him what you're doing wrong. And the only clear answer will be, "We're not working on your timetable. Have faith. Carry on." And you're kind of comforted by that, even though things are not working out when you think they should.

12. There are generous people everywhere; and sometimes even the smallest gestures of love or kindness will make you weep. It can truly be overwhelming. Whether you receive of somebody's money or time or words of confidence, you feel known. And you wish you could adequately express your love and gratitude to these individuals, who have fast become your favorite people ever.

13. When you least expect it, you will receive clarity. For example, maybe you're in the temple. And maybe there's a man in front of you who has cerebral palsy and it takes his every painstaking effort to move ever so slowly, with the help of a walker. And you notice the grimace in his face, and the slowness of his breath. And it surprises you to see he's younger than you. And a temple worker looks to you, wondering if you have come with this man to the temple today in order to assist him. And you haven't, but you find yourself placing your hand on this stranger's back and asking if he needs any help. And his grimace turns into a wide and warm smile, and he chuckles and responds, "Oh...I

need every kind of help." And as you are drawn into his disarming laughter, you marvel at his disposition and his faith and optimism. And you are embarrassed at how whiny you've been about your own temporary struggles. And you feel a voice patiently whispering to you, gently reminding you, "Your trial is a moment. Endure it well."

~

Forgive, Mend, Repeat

Written December 11, 2006

In the summer of 1988, as a shocking reaction to my dad's midlife crisis that he insisted he was not having, our family moved to the tiny Hawaiian island of Molokai. People have two reactions when they hear about Molokai: 1) Never heard of it, and 2) Wait, isn't that where the lepers are?

You are correct on both accounts. The beaches are beautiful, and the island smells terrific, but it is not a tourist destination – as there is very little to do there. No shopping, no movie theaters, no recreational centers, no stop lights, no cable TV. Just like the pioneers! But with coconuts and ukuleles!

I made a wonderful friend that year named Ann Marie. We were not romantically involved. We did not date, we were not flirtatious, we were not even affectionate. (If you're going to press me for details, I will tell you that occasionally we high-fived.) But she was a wonderful friend who laughed at my jokes, let me play my CDs for her, and shared my distain for this Hawaiian concoction called "poi." (And yes, those were my three prerequisites for friendship.)

At the end of that year, I left for college in Provo, Utah, and Ann Marie stayed on Molokai, where she had one remaining year of high school. We would occasionally write letters, as email or texting hadn't been invented yet. I KNOW! I actually had to dip a quill in ink and write by hand! Just like the pioneers! But with lined paper and contemporary postage stamps!

Then one day, I was careless with Ann Marie's feelings. I'd heard a bizarre rumor, assumed she started it, and I wrote an unfair, accusatory letter that hurt her feelings. It wasn't my intent, really, but I was insensitive, and after I sent it, I immediately regretted it. I wished I could un-send it. I got my quill and ink back out and wrote a letter of apology, forthwith! But I didn't hear back from her. I called her home, but I could never catch her there. I wrote another letter. But it again went unanswered. I actually never, ever heard back from her.

I soon left on my mission for The Church of Jesus Christ of Latter-day Saints, serving in Portugal. And I'll tell you this: When you are inviting people to follow Jesus Christ, you become acutely aware of your own failings at following Him. Missions are places where your weaknesses and shortcomings feel like they are placed directly under a microscope so you can get a good, long look at them. Over time, I felt worse. I suppose one reason that I felt incredibly awful was that for Ann Marie, I was the face of the Church. She knew it was important to me and she had even talked with the missionaries and expressed interest in what I believed. But now, as her friend, I had been un-Christian with her feelings. I wrote several letters to her while I was on my mission, but with never a single response.

While I was in Portugal, my family moved from Hawaii back to the mainland, and I returned from my mission to their new home in Lake

Tahoe, Nevada. Soon after, I returned to school in Provo. Life got busy and I became focused on studying and dating, though not in that order.

Then, in December 1994, during the *First Presidency Christmas Devotional*, President Howard W. Hunter counseled "This Christmas, mend a quarrel. Seek out a forgotten friend. Forgo a grudge. Forgive an enemy. Apologize. Try to understand. Examine your demands on others. Be kind. Be gentle. Laugh a little more. Express your gratitude." (*Ensign, December 2002 Gifts of Christmas.*)

I was reminded of Ann Marie, and how those broken and unresolved feelings from four years prior were still there. I knew I needed to reach out. I knew I needed to express to her that I was wrong. I needed her to hear me say the words.

President Hunter's counsel would return to my mind each Christmas; and finally, after another ten years, I found Ann Marie.

By this time, technology in general, and the Internet, specifically, had advanced into The Thing We Could Not Live Without. And while social media was still years away, there was a tool that could help you stalk people. My friends, I give you Yahoo People Search. I couldn't find Ann Marie, but I did find a mutual friend, Leilani, still living on Oahu, and practicing law.

I called Leilani's work number and got a hold of her! We chatted for a while, catching up on the past several years. Eventually, I asked her if she kept in touch with Ann Marie.

"Nah," she responded. "You know, we went to different colleges, and then after she married George and moved away, we really didn't stay in touch."

"Right…right…" I responded, pretending to know all of these things had happened. "What was George's last name again?" She told me, and

I continued, "Right…right…and where did they move to?" She told me again. "Interesting," I said, suddenly aware that I could soon be having a conversation with Ann Marie.

I hung up with Leilani, browsed the Internet, and found my final clue. Ann Marie's phone number. Right there for public consumption. With Christmas music in the background and President Hunter's ringing endorsement running through my head, I picked up the phone and called. Somebody answered.

"Hello?"

"Ann Marie?"

"Yes."

"Ann Marie…that used to live on Molokai?"

"That's right."

I was so nervous; I could hear myself sweating.

"Sorry, I must have the wrong number," and I hung up.

No, I didn't really do that. But I wanted to. Now that I had found her, what if she decided that I was not worth forgiving? What if she was as embarrassed as I was, and didn't want to talk about it? What if she just plain hung up on me?

"This is Ken Craig." I half-swallowed.

"Oh. My. Word!" she kindly gasped.

And it went from there. Who we married, how many kids we had, where we lived, how we got there, what were our feelings on the then-popular phenomenon of "boy bands." Essentially, summing up our lives from over the past fourteen years. And then the moment came. I reached deep within me and found the intestinal fortitude to begin.

"Hey … I called because I wanted to tell you how much I appreciated your friendship during a time in my life when things were unfamiliar and uncertain. You made things comfortable and fun. You were a wonderful friend. And I know that years ago, in a moment of being young and stupid, I said something hurtful. I don't remember what it was, but I wish I could take it back. And I am so sorry that I ever said it."

And then she said it.

"Oh…it's ok. I forgive you."

I could literally feel a physical shift. A change. After years and years of longing for forgiveness – a forgiveness that seemed virtually unattainable – I felt a chapter of my life close with redemption.

Was I now a better person? Probably not. Had I hurt other people's feelings in the last fourteen years and not even been aware of it? Probably. Do I currently owe apologies to friends and family members that surround me? Most likely. Why was this specific occurrence different? I don't know. But I had felt spiritually nudged over the years to make it right. And to have the opportunity to do so meant more than I can say.

Nothing else really changed after that. We don't live near each other nor do we casually call to see how the other's family is doing. But whenever we exchange Christmas cards or reach out over social media or wish each other a happy birthday, I feel the spirit of asking for and receiving forgiveness. And I'm better for it.

When Showing Up Comes Full Circle

Written April 30, 2019

I was serving in a bishopric in Las Vegas, Nevada in the fall of 2005. For those unfamiliar with the administrative structure of a ward (or congregation) in The Church of Jesus Christ of Latter-day Saints, a bishopric is made up of a bishop and two counselors that work alongside him, helping direct the work and efforts within a ward organization, and usually serving as the butt of the joke where they are forced to do the hula at the annual ward luau. Often, the congregation is referred to informally as a "ward family." And I'll be honest, I love this term.

I don't think I'd lived an especially sheltered life up to this point, but I realize now I had successfully avoided a lot of trauma. Unless you count the unfortunate week in 1978 where, as a 7-year-old, I spent every afternoon romping in a pile of dirt that had mysteriously appeared on the side of our house, next to what would eventually become our garden – only to finally be informed by my dad that, in fact, it was not dirt, but a steaming mountain of manure. I still shudder.

But during that November in 2005, my heart broke in a new way. The Boyens, a family within our "ward family," unexpectedly lost their wife and mother, Lisa. It was the first time I remember receiving news that literally made me feel like I had the wind knocked out of me.

Craig and Lisa Boyens, with their kids Bentley (age 14), Bailey (age 10), Chloe (age 5), and Ava (age 3), had moved from San Diego the year before. They were effortlessly likeable, with an easygoing approach to life, parenting, and hairstyles. I loved being around them.

Craig and Lisa were out one evening, at a concert, when without warning, Lisa suffered a brain aneurysm and passed away. As a husband and father, I could not stop thinking about Craig. I felt lost *for* him. I was so unsure of how I would navigate such a situation; I couldn't imagine how he or anyone could do it. I also felt a heightened awareness of the oldest Boyens child, Bentley.

Bentley was sort of living in a lawless frontier. With his dad needing to work to provide for the family, Bentley ran the show at home. I didn't live in the Boyens home, so I don't know for *sure* what the day to day life looked like for a household led by a 14-year-old young man with no parents around, but I've seen enough John Hughes movies to *kind of* know what it looked like. I at least know what it would have looked like when *I* was 14.

But miraculously, that Boyens ship kept sailing. I'm confident there were rough waters. I am positive there were arguments and frustrated nights and feelings of inadequacy and misunderstandings and loneliness and hours of television and an abundance of Taco Bell wrappers … but we didn't see it. (Well, I may have regularly stumbled upon Taco Bell wrappers. But that was it.)

Not only did the Boyens home remain intact, but it became a gathering place. It was a safe landing spot where people marinated in love. Craig was a genuine cheerleader for the friends of his children, and Bentley himself seemed to draw people into his circle.

Serving in a bishopric, first as a counselor then as bishop, it was my privilege to spend a lot of time with Bentley as he grew up. I discovered early on that one of my favorite things about Bentley is his ability to be a natural leader based on one single trait: he is inclusive. As I watched Bentley grow from ages 14 to 19, I think everyone he met thought they were his best friend, including my son, who Bentley taught in a primary class at church. Several of Bentley's friends from school were baptized into The Church of Jesus Christ of Latter-day Saints, because of his example and love for them. It became almost a catch phrase for Bentley, that every time he walked away from someone, or even a group of people, he would call out, without irony or sarcasm, "I love you." Throughout his youth, Bentley was full of hope and optimism. He had incredible faith, and it was evident just by how he lived.

I frequently met with Bentley during youth activities and interviews. He was regularly in my home. We would travel together for youth summer outings. I admired his unassuming strength and appreciated his friendly nature. I was incredibly interested in his future and his well-being. I wanted to offer something extra to Bentley, some new hope or reassurance that he'd see his mom again and that somehow, she was aware of him now. But he already knew. There were no words that were going to make everything better. We all knew it. It seemed that simply showing up and letting him know I loved him was all he ever needed or wanted.

Bentley turned 19 and left to serve a mission in Tucson, Arizona for The Church of Jesus Christ of Latter-day Saints. Shortly after he returned, I was released as the bishop of the ward, and my family and I moved to Utah. I would occasionally reach out to Bentley and ask if he ever considered moving up north. And eventually, he did. I'd like to take credit for that, but it was just a matter of timing and Bentley following his own impressions and life path.

I was thrilled, though. It meant getting to see him from time-to-time. And one of those times was when he showed up to Katie's birthday party ... with this beautiful, bright, smiley soul named Andrea. Not being socially sensitive at all, I asked, out loud and directly in front of both of them, if they were "serious." Because if you'd seen them, you guys, you'd understand. You would have done precisely the same thing. It was one of those moments where you saw two people together and they suddenly just made all the sense in the world. They looked like they belonged. And both of them, with all the grace in the world, answered me back, "Yeah, probably. I guess. This is our third date." They seemed so comfortable and so confident. I was so thrilled for them.

Throughout the coming months, we got to spend time with them. We spent holidays together, movie premiers, lunches. We were all just waiting for the inevitable, and grateful we were invited along for the ride. It was like watching the longest rom-com *ever*. We knew how the story was going to end, but the suspense was tortuous!

And finally, that next summer, they got married in San Diego. We were privileged to be there, and it was beautiful. Two years later, they had a lovely baby girl named Mia. Another two years later, they had gorgeous baby Ellie. And I got to be right there, watching this amazing family grow. I got to see Bentley slide into adulthood and grow into this loving father and adoring husband. And I was so proud of him.

Then, this past spring, my dad suddenly and unexpectedly passed away. He wasn't old, he wasn't sick. It was just his time, I suppose. And my heart ached at losing him. I stayed with my mom for several days. I immediately missed my dad and felt this weight of worry for my mom. I had never lost a parent before. It seemed odd to me to watch the rest of the world move on, as if the world hadn't just completely changed. As if everything were the same and the world didn't know that this marvelous person was no longer here with us. I kind of didn't understand that and kind of didn't like it. And those were the thoughts going through my head as I left my mom and traveled back home.

I was sitting in my bedroom when Katie walked in and said, "There's someone here to see you." Not sure I felt like seeing anyone, I carefully walked into the living room. And there was Bentley. Bentley with his beautiful family. I thought about how almost 14 years ago I was sitting with Bentley, after he lost his mom. I thought about all the times I sat with him, wishing I had something to say or give that would fix everything, but hoping that just being with him would provide *something*. And now, here he was, returning the favor.

After several hugs between all of us, we sat on the couches in the front room. My kids had piled into the room and dumped a basket of plastic Easter eggs onto the floor to entertain Mia. The room was full of people I loved. We spoke a little, with full hearts. Nobody pretended to understand all the feelings or have all the words, but I felt especially loved because Bentley, who was uniquely qualified to understand some of what I was feeling, had come to share himself with me.

They shared convictions and testimony and love. I felt the Lord's awareness of me through Bentley and Andrea. I felt our lives kind of weaved together again in a heartbreaking, wonderful way. It felt a little bit like heaven in my living room.

WHEN I WAS A CHILD, I SPAKE AS A CHILD … AND KIND OF STILL DO

"What I look forward to is continued immaturity followed by death."

– Dave Berry

Highly Defective

Written November 5, 2007

I recently attended a luncheon/convention (lunchvention?) where the internationally celebrated and unreservedly bald Stephen R. Covey spoke. You may recognize him from such acclaimed work as *The 7 Habits of Highly Effective People* and *How to Roll Around in a Pile of Your Own Money*.

The reason for his recent tour is to promote his new book, *The 8th Habit*. I haven't read it yet, but there is something very Disney-esque about it. If there are eight habits of highly effective people, shouldn't that eighth habit have been included in the first book? It's like when you buy *Cinderella* on DVD, and then a few months later – Oh, didn't we tell you? Now there's *Super Deluxe Chrome Plated Forever Enchanted Cinderella*. And it comes with a real pumpkin that turns into a real carriage for riding to the royal ball!

In any case, Mr. Covey is regarded as one of the most brilliant minds in leadership authority, organizational consulting, family unity, and using money for kindling. The man is universally respected, unanimously adored, and abundantly revered. When he speaks, people listen.

I've actually had the opportunity to attend quite a few luncheons lately, with speakers who are considered the authority in their field, ranging from topics such as the Middle East to finance to land development to embezzlement. (Yes, he served time, and yes, he now works for the government.) And after sitting through a few of these, I began to wonder what it would be like to be sought after as these folks are. To be considered the very last word on a subject.

Feeling derisory and somewhat inept, I tried to fathom a subject where people might consider me the quintessential expert. "Oh," someone would say whilst munching on a Reuben at the country club, "you want to know everything there is to know about (X)? You've got to hear Ken Craig's take on that. Insightful, witty, brilliant. The man knows more about (X) than anybody."

This is all I could come up with:

The Subtleties of Flirting. (This is a stretch, as I am way, way out of practice. Unless you count my feeble attempts at wooing Katie by pinching her bum and changing song lyrics to make them "suggestive.")

B-List Actors from the 80s. (I know them all. This includes Lisa Welchel as Blair from *Facts of Life*, and Marc Price as *Family Ties'* Skippy.)

Staying Awake on Road Trips.

Making it Look Like You Are Shuffling Through the Pantry to Make Dinner When You Are, In Fact, Stealthily Eating Oreos Right in Front of Your Unsuspecting Kids.

Using Your DVR to Watch One Hour TV Episodes in 20 Minutes or Less. (Provided you're interested only in plot – not commercials, not character development, not embarrassingly bad dialogue. And certainly not dancing "stars.")

That's about all I could come up with. No highly effective habits, no groundbreaking insight into world peace, no theories of how Las Vegas will run out of water long before it runs out of liquor. But I am qualified to write a book Mr. Covey hasn't considered. *7 Moderately Effective Ways to Flirt with Your Wife*. Chapter 1: The Use of Alternate Song Lyrics.

No. 1 Juror

Written February 7, 2009

Please don't be jealous, but earlier this week, my county needed me, and – that's right – I answered the call. Recognizing I was uniquely qualified, and quick to respond to the cry of justice, I carefully tore along the calculated, perforated lines of my jury duty summons.

No sooner had I read through the form letter when I noticed that this letter contained both blue AND red ink! Clearly, this was of utmost importance. I called Katie over and sat her down on the couch. I wasn't entirely sure of how I was going to explain this to her. I mean, after 13 years of marriage, I'm sure she thought she knew everything there was to know about me. But how could she know that my sense of justice and mercy was so acute, that our nation's court system (well, our county's court system, but I digress) was not only hanging by a thread – but a thread that I held in the palm of my hand?

Thankfully, she was supportive. In fact, she almost acted like it wasn't a big deal. She kind of brushed it off and went back to making dinner. SO BRAVE, my little Katie.

As you can imagine, I had a lot of preparing to do. I quickly went to Barnes & Noble and bought all the Grisham they had. (I was going to just go to the county library for the books, but – call me a conspiracy theorist – county library, county court? I'm sure they are in cahoots. It just seemed better to avoid the entire situation. That is exactly how they trip you up.)

I also rented the Pauley Shore film noir, *Jury Duty*, and studied the process, so as to not miss a single nuance. I couldn't follow it initially; but after the third viewing, I began piecing it together. Brilliant.

I then decided to make an iPod mix of court room music. But all I could think of was the theme music from *Law & Order*; so I just looped it and carry it with me wherever I go. I walk with more purpose, now. But not necessarily a quicker walk, because then my iPod earpiece keeps falling out.

And finally, I began using lines from courtroom dramas, and other such trash talk. And this has really helped. For example, when I drive up to the ATM and it says it's "Out of Order," I scream, "No, YOU'RE out of order! This whole BANK is out of order!" And sometimes, at my day job (insurance), I have clients who ask, "Do you think I have enough insurance, honestly?" And I have to answer, "You can't HANDLE my honesty!" And then, just for good measure, when my kids promise me good behavior so that I will do some favor for them, I say, "Your mouth is writing checks your body can't cash!" And, well, thanks to all my preparation, I have actually been invited to "call backs" (courtroom/theater speak) for this very high-profile case. I wish I could tell you about it; but my ability to keep secrets is probably another reason my county sought me out as they did. And I can't turn my back on them now. They need me. Plus, this may be my only opportunity to ever do my Samuel L. Jackson's, "Yes, they deserve to die, and I hope they burn in he@#!"

~

Kid Praise

Written February 16, 2009

Normally, I'm pretty skeptical about any new-age pop-psychology mumbo jumbo slapped onto a magnet and strategically placed front and center on a refrigerator. However, I recently came across one such attention-grabbing propaganda, and I have to admit, I was intrigued.

It read: *101 Ways to Praise Kids.*

It was produced by some company that goes by the name of Nannies & Housekeepers U.S.A. At first I was discouraged, as it appeared that it was something solely created for nannies, which we don't have because a) we don't have the money, and b) there is only one Mary Poppins, and I don't think she's available. But although it was targeted at nannies, I couldn't help wondering if it might work for parents too, as they sometimes interact with their own children as well.

I gave it a shot.

I've carried it around in my pocket for a week now, and I've really noticed a difference in my children's confidence. Used to be that when they ran up to tell me something or had accomplished something, I just didn't know how to react. But now I do!

I tried it out on Abbie first.

Abbie: Dad, I made eight loaves of bread today.

Me: (Scanning the card for the right thing to say) You're a pleasure to know! (Nailed it.)

Connor: Dad, I drew this picture for you.

Me: What a great listener!

Tanner: Dad, I had an accident when I couldn't climb up on the toilet fast enough.

Me: You've earned my respect!

Becca: Pffffpts.

Me: Thanks for caring!

Garren: Dad, in Cub Scouts we talked about coin collections.

Me: The time you put in really shows!

Roxanna: (And I wish I were making this one up…) Dad, listen to the song I memorized from *West Side Story*! "My daddy beats my mommy; my mommy clobbers me; my grandpa is a commie; my grandma pushes tea; my sister wears a mustache; my brother wears a dress! Goodness! Gracious! That's why I'm a mess!"

Me: Class act!

So, turns out, as you can plainly see, that sometimes this stuff really works! I can really tell a difference in my children's attitudes. In fact, I'd go so far as to say that if this parenting thing doesn't work out, I could totally be a nanny. Kenny Poppins.

Heated Debates

Written July 30, 2012

As a result of being crazy from the summer heat, Katie and I have recently had two "animated discussions." I'm going to tell you about them right now; but please, do not judge Katie too harshly.

The first started in our family van. Our ten-year old, Connor, was sitting on the bench directly behind the driver and passenger seats. I was driving, Katie was co-pilot. I could see Connor getting restless, so decided to engage him in a lively discussion.

"Connor, if you could have just one superpower, what would it be?" I asked as I looked back over my shoulder at him.

"Flying," he responded without much contemplation.

"That's correct," I answered, facing forward again.

"I don't think I would pick 'flying,'" Katie casually throws out. She had her oversized-lens sunglasses on.

"Of course you would."

"Why 'of course'?"

"Because as an entire UNIVERSE we have already agreed that FLYING is the number one superpower that EVERYBODY would want. It's, like, in the Constitution."

"Not for me," she states flatly and nestles into her headrest. As if the discussion is over.

"WHAT ARE YOU SAYING TO ME?"

"I'm saying I wouldn't choose 'flying.' I think I would choose to be 'extra strong.'"

"Extra strong?! That's the worst superpower EVER!"

"What if I got in a fight?"

"THEN YOU COULD FLY AWAY IF FLYING WAS YOUR SUPERPOWER! As a Christian, on principle, don't you think it would be more appropriate to fly away than to hurt somebody?"

"...and think of the handy things I could do around the house if I were stronger!"

"I can do those things for you – and I am naturally ripped!" (This was really the only faulty claim in my entire defense.)

"Then maybe I would want 'the power to read minds.'"

"Everybody has that power. It's called 'reading Facebook.' It's not that great."

"I just don't think I would choose 'flying.'"

"It's like I don't know you at all... And we have seven children together."

So, not that it's a competition, but I clearly won that "debate," right? Right? Rest of the world that knows "flying" is the obvious superpower of choice? Thank you.

This second one is a little dicier. And it's because it's personal. See, when Katie and I got married, I had, give or take, one krafillion cds and mixed tapes. Katie had one. And it was one I had given her. So, when it comes to music, that's just my territory. And we have been in agreement on this from the very beginning. Like, on our first date. THAT beginning.

So you can imagine my surprise when Katie, sitting at the computer desk scrolling iTunes, states, "We have too many C+C Music Factory songs."

"What?" I answer from the couch, looking up from my book.

"We have far, far too many C+C Music Factory songs."

Now, just like the rest of America, I am aware of precisely two C +C Music Factory songs. "Gonna Make You Sweat" and … you know…the other one. And I am going to plead guilty that I have compilation cds and stuff that I purchased in college and beyond that I've randomly loaded into iTunes, so I am not completely aware of all the songs that I have in there. But I am not going to sit idly by and let Katie give me the business regarding our music collection.

"There's no such thing as too many C+C Music Factory songs," I confidently shoot back.

"Eight?" she says.

EIGHT?! What the WHAT?! Where in the far reaches of this world did eight C+C Music Factory songs come from, and how did they get on my computer?!

"Those are eight classics," I defend myself.

"They all sound exactly the same," she says, succinctly nailing it on the head.

"No, they don't. I like all of them, separately."

"Name them."

Oh, BABY. She was laying down the gauntlet. And I was going to lose. THIS is why I should have my cell phone on me at all times. I could have strategically looked this up with the phone behind my book.

I looked back at her, and in complete desperation, tried to give her one of those "Isn't this a bit childish?" looks. This, of course, blew up in my face because she accurately read it for what it was – a bluff.

She raised her left eyebrow, inviting me to begin.

"Well, there's 'Gonna Make You Sweat'…"

"Yes…."

"And then there's 'Everybody Dance Now'…"

"That's the same song."

"Mmmm…I don't think so."

"Yes, it says it right here, 'Gonna Make You Sweat,' then parentheses, 'Everybody Dance Now.'"

"Oh…well, the 'Everybody Dance' Now that I'm referring to was a b-side that was released only in Europe, so…maybe it's not one of the songs that we have, but it is most certainly one of their songs, so…"

Stone-faced: "What are the names of the other seven songs?"

"Right. Uhm…I don't remember the name, but it says something about, "I'm just a squirrel, trying to get a nut –"

"That's the same song," Katie rudely interrupts.

"You sure?"

"Yes."

"Hmmmm….OH! 'Here We Go, Let's Rock & Roll!'" I say, a little too excited about knowing a second C+C song, making it more obvious I have no idea what I'm talking about.

"OK. What else?"

"…can you give me a hint?" I ask, defeat looming.

"Starts with a Things that Make You…"

"OH! 'Things That Make You Go Hmmm.'"

"That's only three songs you've named."

"Yes," I begin, with a new strategy. "But those three sound distinctly different. I am right about those. But you are right about the other five, because I think those five sound the same as these three, and they are totally unnecessary. You know what? I'm having another thought – since I'm in charge of the music – why don't we just delete those other five, because, as you said, they sound too similar to the three, very distinct, very original songs that I just listed. So, you were right, and I was right. But let's not argue anymore about who is right, and who shouldn't be talking about whether or not our music library has enough or not enough of something. Right?"

Whew. So, we'll call that one a tie.

But seriously, if this heat doesn't fade soon, there's going to be a whole-lotta discussions about some other urgent and topical issues that are severely affecting our marriage. Like when we start discussing my tendency to watch a *Seinfeld* rerun on TV when Katie points out that we literally own the DVD and could watch it anytime, especially at a decent hour? Oh, you don't want to a front row seat to that show, folks.

My Dignity on the Conveyer Belt

Written April 26, 2011

So, it's 9:00 p.m., and I'm in the Express Lane at our friendly neighborhood Albertsons. I wasn't planning to be out, so I'm dressed quite casually. *Quite* casually. Very, extremely casually. If I were dressed any more casually, I'd be in the shower.

I have my Ten Items or Less on the conveyer belt, and I'm waiting my turn, when I hear voices and glance over my shoulder to see who's behind me. Lo and behold, it's Brother Dustin Hoffman* and his little daughter. (* name has been changed.) Brother Hoffman is in the bishopric of a neighboring ward in our stake, and I've known him – more as an acquaintance, really – for about three years. My wife and I spoke at a fireside in his ward a couple of years back, and afterwards he invited us to go to dinner with him and his wife sometime. (P.S. We never went.) And since I've been in our bishopric, I've seen him at various and sundry meetings where we've chatted casually from time to time; so, while I wouldn't call us "friends," I'd say we are definitely "friendly."

But not tonight.

First, I'm very self-conscious because I'm dressed like I've wandered from my bed to the bathroom, and second, well, Brother Hoffman has caught me – ME, a bishop – engaged in the reading of an intriguing article out of the cheap and tawdry publication known as *People Magazine*.

"Oh, hey!" I nervously call over my shoulder to Brother Hoffman, as I fumble with the magazine and try to hide it behind a copy of *Newsweek*. (Why a single copy of *Newsweek* was on the "impulse buy" rack – the same rack as *People* – is beyond me, and my only explanation is that blessings come in all shapes and sizes.)

Brother Hoffman pipes up, and in full confidence says, "Hey Robert! I almost didn't recognize you."

Now, for those of you keeping score at home…there's a good reason Brother Hoffman almost didn't recognize me. My name is not Robert. Never has been. But I'm not really in a chit-chatty mood, don't have any real reason to correct him, and now I don't have to worry about being judged for my recreational reading as an added bonus. So, I don't say anything. I just wave and turn back to face the cashier, who is helping the person in front of me. But Brother Hoffman can't leave good enough alone.

"I didn't know you lived on this side of town?" he says.

Ah, nuts. I'm stuck in line and I'm being dragged into chitchat. And I'm at a slight disadvantage, because I'm suddenly a fictional character with a background that only Brother Hoffman knows.

"Yeah…yeah. Live over off Sarsaparilla. How about you? You still in the Elkhorn Springs Second Ward?"

Brother Hoffman cocks his head back, and while his smile stays intact, there's suddenly a question behind it. "Yes…" he slowly answers. And it occurs to me that Robert is most likely not a Latter-day Saint and wouldn't know that Brother Hoffman is in a "ward."

"Oh," I say. "Great." And now I've got to quickly strike up conversation to distract him before he says, "You aren't Robert, are you? Why didn't you say so? What's wrong with ya, boy?"

So, I say, "Yep, we just moved, actually, and now we live just one street over from your sister, Destiny Child*." (* name has been changed.)

Strike Two. Apparently, Robert doesn't know Destiny, and may not even know that Brother Hoffman has a sister. He is just staring at me now – a long, quiet, blank stare. I'm starting to panic. I feel like he's about to point at me and say, "That's him, officer, that's him. I'm positive. That's the impostor that was reading *People* in the Express Lane at Albertsons!"

The longer the moment lasts, the more I anticipate him calling my bluff. I start to do a character sketch in my mind. Who is this Robert? Would he buy gum? Should I put some on the conveyer belt? Would he be reading celebrity gossip? Should I ask Brother Hoffman his feelings about the Reynolds/Johansson split? Is that something Robert would do? Does Robert swear? Probably not in front of little girls, so that option is out. I've got to think! The tension is so thick; you could cut it up and sell it in the Albertsons bakery at $8 a slice.

Finally, when my face is about to burst through my forehead, the cashier speaks up. "Sir," she says to Brother Hoffman. "Sir, would you mind tying that cord up behind you? I'm closing the lane. You'll be my last customer."

"Oh, sure," he says. "That's easier than having to tell the person behind me that you're closed and won't help them."

"Yeah," I chime in, "the last thing you want is to be trapped in an uncomfortable situation." Inside I think I am the funniest man alive, but my face is stone cold, as if there is no irony in my comment.

Finally, it is my turn at the register. I am almost home free. The cashier asks for my special "Albertsons Card" that gives me fabulous discounts and incredible cash savings, which I gladly hand over. Once the card is in her hand, however, I recall that their canned response whenever they swipe my card is "Thank you, Kenneth." NO! Their polite, new-age customer service mumbo-jumbo is going to completely foul up my escape!

I start to weigh my options. One, I can correct the cashier, "Oh, it's 'Robert Kenneth,' actually. But the 'Robert' is silent." Or, "Oh, that's funny, I have my twin brother's Albertsons card. Hmm – this happens all the time. Do you know my twin? He's in the Elk Ridge bishopric. I think he spoke at a fireside in your ward once with his wife." One thing is for sure; I will quickly sell this cashier down the river before letting Brother Hoffman know that I am not Robert.

Then I start to panic double as I realize that at any second, somebody I know could enter the store and call me by name. What then? Do I deny who I am? If my neighbor walks in and says, "Hey Ken!" do I snub them? Do I look at Brother Hoffman and say, "I think he's talking to you?"

I turn and focus on the cashier. I've got to deal with her first, and once I'm done, I can bolt for the door and run out into the night.

She starts, "Thank you, Ke—"

"No, thank YOU!" I interrupt, grabbing the receipt out of her hand, hoisting my groceries in my other hand, and heading for the door. For the sake of keeping up with appearances, I turn back once more to Brother Hoffman and say, "Have a good night."

"We'll see you later," he says, still looking puzzled. He's not going to let this go away. I can tell right now. I'm just curious if our next meeting will be at Albertsons or at a meeting at church. In the meantime, I am going to have to do some serious research on this Robert guy.

THE ART OF FRUGALITY

"Not everything that can be counted counts, and not everything that counts can be counted."

– Albert Einstein

A Little Off the Top

Written June 5, 2012

With the poop-tacular state of our economy, we are always looking for innovative ways to save a few bucks around the Craig house. And at this point, we have moved far beyond the obvious choices of eliminating superfluous magazine subscriptions (take a hike, *Reader's Digest*), indulgent video streamlining (hasta la vista, Netflix), and unnecessary food purchases (I never liked you anyway, vegetables).

One creative cost-cutting initiative: Home haircuts, a la my wife, Katie. Katie never went to haircutting school, but she doesn't let that bother her. She can do our boys' haircuts in a matter of moments, as they all look quite handsome with what the haircutting industry terms as "buzz cuts." (I apologize if my use of haircutting jargon is confusing.)

My hair, however, is a completely different animal. A dangerous animal. A quickly graying, sometimes stubborn, porcupine of an animal. And while I think Katie is quite good at cutting it, her desire for a mane of perfection guarantees it is by no means a quick procedure.

But I don't mind the length of her process. Sitting still for that long allows time for innuendo and bum-grabbing (conducted by yours truly), sharing of stories that we may have forgotten to tell each other that week, and reflection, generally brought on by the fact that I'm shirtless and staring into our bathroom mirror at my 41-year-old body, wondering what the crap has happened.

"I used to play water polo in high school," I begin the conversation.

"Yep … (Katie snaps the No. 3 clip onto the razor) … you've told me."

"I'm just saying … you know … there was a time when you could have washed laundry on these abs … instead of … whatever … dishes, I guess."

"You look just fine," she assures me.

"HOW ARE YOU EVEN ATTRACTED TO ME?" I question.

"You're very attractive," she responds, not looking at me while she snaps off the No. 3 from the razor. "Now, did you want me to shave your back while I've got this out?"

I pout silently for a while, thoughtfully considering that perhaps our bodies resurrect at their age-18 version. Then Katie pulls me out of my funk with a story.

"Did I tell you that Becca has been singing to herself when she's sitting on the toilet?" We laugh and then it's my turn. "Did I tell you about the check-out lady at Walmart that told me if I was going to buy this much produce then I should probably shop somewhere else?" Then we discuss our strategy to own beach-front property and be independently wealthy someday, and it's awesome.

So, then we're feeling all lovey-dovey and I'm already only half-dressed, so of course I turn on the charm and start in with the innuendo. We're in close proximity, alone, AND awake, so all three elements of "romance" are in the air. With scissors in her hand, me sitting on a bucket, and bits of hair all over both of us, I start singing the Righteous Broth-er's "Unchained Melody" and, as you can imagine, the scene looks exactly like … well, whatever the opposite of Patrick Swayze and Demi Moore is.

Sometime later Katie takes a step back, squints at my head, and closely examines her work. She's her toughest critic. When she's finally satisfied, I jump in the shower and sing to her while she sweeps up the hair. For some reason, more than almost anything else we do together, this moment makes me feel like we are already 82 years-old and there are no stories we don't know about each other and we just enjoy the fact that it's us, in all our glorious and unsightly details.

I guess I don't mind all the effects of our lackluster economy.

May I Axe you a Question?

Written April 29, 2010

For those of you who know me well, you know I'm a pretty conventional kind of a feller. I wear a suit to church on Sundays, I shower every day, and I never drive slow in the fast lane. I even use all the correct grammar and punctuation when I text, for crying-gosh-sakes-out-loud. Bottom line: I'm as socially and hygienically moderate as it gets.

So obviously, I have no business purchasing, much less wearing this very special concoction: AXE Body Spray – Dark Temptation.

I know, I know. Who do I think I am? I should have just kept my nose clean and stayed to my side of the aisle. Right Guard, Old Spice…maybe even Mitchum if I were feeling adventurous. But AXE? What am I, auditioning for an MTV reality series? *Old Dudes Not Acting Their Age!* Or *America's Next Top Delusional Father of Six.* I don't own any gold chains and I'm not personal friends with any club owners. What am I doing?

And not just AXE, but DARK TEMPTATION!

But hear me out. See, I figure that if there is a body part in need of some serious help in being considered tempting … ladies and gentlemen, I give you … the armpit.

So now, when I get all dolled up for a night out with Katie, I gots everything a-workin' for me. Oh, yeaaaaahhhhh. Salt n' pepper hair? Check. Pants? Check. T-shirt? Check. (What? Were we going someplace nice?) Pocket change? Check. 2005 Toyota Camry? Check. And now…tempting armpits? Double check. Sorry ladies…I'm spoken for.

To be completely candid, though, I should admit that "tempting armpits" was not the biggest selling point for me. No. It was the tagline "As irresistible as chocolate." Strangely, it comforted me to know that in some post-apocalyptic setting, if all the world was falling apart and food everywhere was predominantly contaminated, and looting was commonplace, and we were on the verge of extinction … I could eat my deodorant. And it would be delicious.

Anyway, I've been wearing/eating it for about a month now. And … nothing. I'd like to start a class action suit against AXE for false advertising, because I am neither more tempting than I was before, nor is my deodorant as satisfying as real, legitimate chocolate. But the good news is I think Katie and I might be candidates for the new reality show now in pre-production: *People Who Believe Everything They Read, and the Women Who Love Them.*

A Good Ol' Fashioned Throw-Down

Written August 29, 2011

What you see above is not a multi-generational photo. No, this is simply Katie's family – the one she grew up with. The Fillmores. You have her parents there, front and center, and then all the siblings (minus one, Robyn, who passed away when she was eight and Katie was 14).

Yes, you've counted that correctly. Ten children. Nine daughters. In a row. I'm just going to let that gel in your mind for a moment.

Though it's contrary to social standards as well as most movie stereo-types and dated stand-up comedian observations, I quite enjoy my in-laws. And I'm always intrigued by how diverse they are. I mean, nine young ladies baked in the same oven and raised in pretty much the same environment … but their approaches to life as well as their passions, in-terests, techniques and leg-shaving habits are as varied as their hairstyles.

However, one thing they do have in common is their universal sub-scription to the frugal mantra "Use it up, wear it out, make it do, or do without." None of these exceptional women have the attitude of "I am entitled to Such-and-Such," or "I deserve Thus-and-So." These are prudent, parsimonious girls.

And while I admire that trait, I will freely admit that what I love most about it is that these cost-conscious attitudes occasionally produce what the Fillmores affectionately refer to as a "Throw-Down."

According to tournament rules, a Throw-Down may occur when three or more of the sisters know they will be together for an evening. It involves the preliminary steps of going through your closets and drawers and bag-ging up whatever clothes you are feeling "done" with. You then lug these clothing items to the Throw-Down location (usually in somebody's living room), and when all are safely gathered in … you hock your wares.

Please note, you are not actually selling your clothing to the highest bidder. Your goal is just to get rid of your clothes, and hopefully head home with armfuls of clothing that your sisters – for whatever reason – are no longer interested in owning themselves. It is essentially a "cloth-ing exchange" party, wherein you are throwing down your old clothes and picking up used clothes that are now new to you.

Simple enough, right? But where the hilarity ensues is here – in the trading of the clothing. See, one of the other traits that the Fillmore

Girls all share is honesty. Or, you might also call it "dismal salesmanship." They wait their turn, then stand before the crowd and present their clothing, like an auctioneer. An auctioneer who, despite his honesty and disdain for the clothing items in his arms, manages to get other people to snatch them up. I have to think that it's because each girl is so enthusiastic and upbeat with their sales pitch, you can't help but want to give it a try! And then try it on immediately in the "changing area," otherwise known as "behind the couch."

Last week all the sisters were together for the first time in many years. The excitement and energy were almost tangible. I could barely contain my giddiness in anticipation of the sales pitches! And it did not disappoint. And for you, I present here some of my favorite quotes, overheard at a Fillmore Throw-Down. (Each one said with mucho enthusiasm and gusto!)

Katie, holding up a straight, red dress: "This dress is super cute, but you can't wear it if you are pregnant … or nursing … or if you've ever had a baby. Or if you are bloated."

"This is cuter than it looks." (And it wasn't.)

"This blouse is nice, but I have a hard time moving my arms in it."

"These pants say 'dry clean only'… but they're not anymore!"

"These pants might fit you … the elastic just isn't good for keeping them on."

Rachel, walking into the room, observing Stephanie holding up an item of clothing, "Hey! Wait, what'd I miss? … YUCK!"

"These are so cute, but they're size 8, so I only wear them when I'm pregnant or just had a baby."

"This is completely out of date. I should have gotten rid of it when it was still in style."

"You could make this jumper into a nice tote bag."

"Here's a good 'wash-the-kitchen-floor' shirt!"

"These pants come with spit-up on them."

"I like that shirt!" "Well, it's got weird sleeves." "Ok, great!"

"This jacket is kind of ratty on the ends."

"When I wore this, people told me I looked like a bell."

"This is so cute … I actually might keep it."

"The pits are a little sour on this one. I'm not even sure why I held on to it."

"This sweater makes you look like a bee … or that you're from Hufflepuff."

"Here's some running shorts. They're Speedo. They kind of feel like a diaper. But they wick away the moisture!"

"Here's a shirt. It's actually a little boys' shirt. But I like the fabric."

"This one just has a couple of holes in it. And the pits have seen better days. But it's a cute shirt, and I wore it a lot."

"This is a shirt Rachel gave me … but I feel like a pumpkin every time I wear it."

"This skirt is nice and long, but you can't walk in it."

"This one is so old that Eve wore it out of the Garden … and in high school."

~

Doin' Time at Costco

Written August 5, 2016

I recently worked a demo booth at my local Costco for two weeks. For reasons. (Well, for one reason, really. To make some extra cash.)

It wasn't on the first draft of my list of Things to Do This Summer; but neither was swim with an alligator, lip sync "Boogie Woogie Bugle Boy" or have an ongoing inner dialogue about the pros and cons of breaking up with Facebook – yet I managed to fit all of these things into this season! I guess I was just feeling productive.

I've worked trade shows numerous times … but this was different. This was Costco. Here are some highlights of two-weeks' worth of observations.

If you stand in Costco long enough, the entire world walks by.

98% of that world already owns a Bosch Mixer.

80% of those who own a Bosch Mixer will yell at you, "I love my Bosch!" Most likely in an attempt to stop you from trying to sell them one.

We live among people who will eat Costco pizza at 10:30 AM.

There are a lot of people at Costco *not dressing their truth*. (Extra points if you get this reference.)

It takes three days of eating samples of pot stickers before you get sick of them.

You can eat endless samples of Brazilian cheese bread, grass-fed beef, and Belgian waffles with Nutella and never get sick of them.

The quickest way to reduce people to animalistic, post-apocalyptic behavior is to offer free samples.

People offering samples don't care how many you eat, from a *supply* point of view. But they will judge you for the sheer amount you consume. They quietly judge you with their eyes. And sometimes not as quietly, with their words.

If you're working a booth, and you don't offer samples, you're a leper and you should be ashamed of yourself.

A genuine smile and "hello" from somebody passing by will absolutely make your day. You will have to exercise the greatest level of restraint to not leave your booth and hug that person and ask them if they'd like to chat for a few minutes over some grass-fed beef.

Standing for eleven hours in one spot is not natural. Your body will hurt. In weird places.

If you walk by a booth and the person working it doesn't at least engage you in eye contact, it is because they have just farted and don't want you to come anywhere near them. (They have to stand there for eleven hours! Cut them some slack! Let's see how YOU do after devouring eleven pot stickers!)

Get your heads out of your phones, guys. Our country's greatest form of entertainment is other people's children. Adorable babies abound in Utah County, yes. But my favorite was the four-year-old who had clearly skipped nap time (since the Tuesday before) and, through tears of rage and screams of inhumanity, was using both hands to pick up every item in the cart and hurl it at the floor as fast as he could, while the parents made a bee-line for the front doors, suddenly losing interest in actually making any purchases. I don't know the back-story of what was happening here, but something tells me it's a tale as old as time.

Speaking of back-stories. I made one up for somebody. My first day on the job, a gentleman rolled his cart over and started asking me some genuine questions about the product I was selling. We talked for several minutes, and I observed the number of items already in his cart. He eventually wandered off. "Nice guy," I thought. About ten minutes later he swung by again and let me know he'd talked to his girlfriend, and she wasn't interested in the product I had. Fine. About two hours later ... he came by again ... I was intrigued. What in the world was this guy doing, loitering in a Costco for hours upon hours in the middle of a work week? And then it dawned on me.

He's casing the joint.

I wondered if I should tell management about this shifty dude, late 40s, Lindsey Buckingham look-a-like, that's clearly looking to move some real merchandise from this place.

Then, several hours later ... he came by *again*. This time, with completely different things in his cart. Like, he had put stuff back (or stolen it) and now had a fresh load of goods in his cart. That's when it dawned on me.

He's a widow.

He lost his wife and has become quite reclusive. He suffers from anxieties and the only thing he really does that makes him feel normal is venturing out to large, busy retail locations.

He can strike up conversations with people and act like he is just your average citizen with a "to do" list. Then it occurs to me. My gosh. This man is me. If I were his age and I lost Katie, *this is what I would become!!!* My heart broke for this guy. I wanted to invite him over for dinner.

Then the next morning … I saw him again. And he had a Costco name badge on. And I realized he was shopper security. And then I was embarrassed. So I decided as long as I was embarrassed, I might as well go binge on Belgian waffles with Nutella until somebody shoos me away.

Aside from people I didn't know, I also bumped into a crazy amount of people I *did* know. Well over 100.

I saw a girl I dated my freshman year in college, 1989. We laughed, played "do you remember the time," and realized we both had 16-year olds that should go out sometime. (Because, you guys, 16-year olds love nothing more than for their parents to get involved in their love life.)

I saw the parents of a girl I dated in 1993. The mom hugged me. She was always so kind.

I saw …

A guy I became friends with at the Missionary Training Center for The Church of Jesus Christ of Latter-day Saints. A guy I hadn't seen since 1990.

Young adults I knew in Las Vegas who now live here and are getting married.

Missionaries I knew in Las Vegas who now live here but aren't getting married.

Good friends who would visit with me for long stretches of time and act super interested in my mixers.

People I used to work with.

People I used to perform improv with in college.

You know my good friend Matt? Well, his mom.

An old mission companion.

A guy I used to play racquetball with in Las Vegas.

Neighbors, old friends, new friends.... you get the picture.

That was really my favorite part of the Costco experience. Seeing people from my past and present, and visiting with them. I know some really wonderful people.

Of course, visiting with them also made it so that I had to explain why I was working a booth at Costco. The real reason was boring and required a longer explanation than I cared to dive into. So I got pretty creative.

"Research."

"I'm just filling in for a friend who's on his lunch break."

"I recently bought the company and I'm interested in discovering public opinion on my own."

"It's always been on my Bucket List to do this, and I know a guy."

"I'm just doing some consulting, and this is a weird part of the gig."

"I'm actually a secret shopper."

"This is just my day job."

"Why did you come over here? Didn't you notice I wouldn't make eye contact with you? No, I don't know what smells vaguely like pot stickers."

BACK IN MY DAY

"Life can only be understood backwards; but it must be lived forwards."

– Soren Kierkegaard

My Most Embarrassing Moment on Record

Written October 14, 2008

One night, while in college, I went out on a first date with a girl named…hmmm… It started with an E. (I cared for her, deeply, as you can see.) Elaine? Elizabeth? Anyway, we were walking through a park, fairly close together, but with our hands in our jacket pockets, as it was a fall evening, and the weather was pleasantly cool. When out of the blue, Ellen (?) says, "Tell me your deepest, darkest secret."

I did not care for this.

Firstly, I had known Ester (?) for about two days. Who was she to demand to know my deepest, darkest secrets? Was I to automatically trust this attractive, though virtually unknown woman at face value? A woman who had not shared her deepest, darkest secret with me? A woman who found it perfectly acceptable to walk through a park and consider it a date? A woman whose name started with an E! (Edie? Electra? Ebony?)

But secondly, and most importantly…I didn't have any deep, dark secrets. Unless you count my extensive Huey Lewis & the News CD collection. (And I don't.)

I'll never know what Edwina (?) was probing for that day. But I have attended a number of social gatherings since then where people play such "get-to-know-you" games where you are required to recount, in great detail, information you would not normally or casually put on display. "Deep, dark" information, as it were. Only now it is masqueraded as "What's your most embarrassing moment?"

Well, I happen to have one.

It was early summer, 1993. If memory serves, Rod Stewart couldn't remember if he'd told us lately that he loved us, Tom Hanks was having difficulty sleeping somewhere in Washington state, and I was dating a lovely young woman from Salem, Utah. Danielle.

With BYU not located too far from Salem, we would occasionally go visit Danielle's family for some dining and dancing. (Mostly dining.)

On this particular weekend, her family's ward, the Salem 374th Ward, was having a barbecue in a nearby canyon. I am a big fan of both barbecues and canyons, so I was excited to go.

It was still early enough in the summer that it was quite cool up the canyon, so there was a roaring fire to take off the chill. I had helped Danielle's little brother get a plate of food, and he went off to sit by his sister on a log by the fire. I got my own plate and, not seeing a place to sit, remained standing as I ate on the other side of the fire, straight across from Danielle and her little brother.

There was really a large turnout of people, and there were conversations taking place all over the camping area; though most people didn't drift too far from the fire. I had chatted with a few pleasant folks, making nice and quashing ramped rumors about our impending engagement.

I was finishing the last of my barbecued chicken and preparing to throw my plate in the fire, when I felt an odd sensation around my... uhm, derriere. It was a hand. At first it was cupping my bum, but then it began to rub it. And rub it. And rub it. It was as if my bum were a lamp, and they were expecting Robin Williams to appear. Alarmed, my eyes searched across the fire for Danielle. Not that it would have been okay if Danielle were doing this to me, but she was really the only familiar person there.

Slowly, as if I were being held at gunpoint, I turned and looked to my left. There, facing away from me...was a total stranger. She was probably mid-forties, long hair, mother of five. And her right hand was now stuffed into the back pocket of my jeans. She had clearly mistaken me for somebody else. For example, her tall, firm-bummed husband. Unsure of what to say, but confident this was going to end no other way than badly, I didn't say anything.

I stood there staring at her, waiting for her to turn and make eye contact with a man who she did not know. A man who was not comfortable with the whereabouts of her hand. A man who did not give this stuff away for free!

Finally, she turned and realized she had been fondling the wrong bum. Oh, the horror in her eyes! The shock! In an effort to defuse the situation and bring some levity to the entire scene before she could speak, I threw my arm around her shoulder and said, "Hey, baby, you coming with me?"

"YOU'RE NOT MY HUSBAND!"

Well, she had found her voice. The entire ward stopped and turned. Wards from neighboring canyon barbecue parties stopped and turned. Yes, in addition to roving hands, this woman had some lungs. But now, while her stating of the obvious should have incriminated her, I suddenly look like the visiting sick-o from outside the ward, who has been going around shoving people's hands into my back pockets.

Well, we all had a good laugh, she decided to go back to her husband, and I never went back to visit Danielle's family – or their ward.

~

The Stake Dance: The Metaphor for Life

Written August 16, 2011

Without permission, my daughter Abbie turned 14 last week. And I have no one to blame but myself, as it even happened on my watch, and I did absolutely nothing to stop it. In my defense, I was distracted by my life-changing AppleTV and being able to watch YouTube videos on my television! Ah, technology. I kind of fear you, sometimes.

The thing about being 14 in The Church of Jesus Christ of Latter-day Saints is that you now get to experience that rite of passage known as … The Stake Dance. And Abbie will be attending her first on Saturday.

(For you who are not of this faith, a standard congregation in the Latter-day Saint Church is called a "ward." Several wards combine to make up a "stake." And once a month a dance is held in one of the ward buildings for all the youth, ages 14 to 18 in the entire stake. It's a marvelous social opportunity for the young people in today's world to come be together so they can bask in the overpowering odiferous combination of cologne and body order, circumvent actual conversations by texting each other from opposite ends of the gym, and at all costs – including death first – avoid any actual dancing.)

My gosh, what an emotional rollercoaster a Saturday night stake dance used to be for me. It was like experiencing puberty in a microwave. In one single evening you were terrified, elated, awkward, euphoric ... you loved everyone, you hated everyone, wished you were younger, wished you were older, you had the sweats, and by night's end ... your voice had changed, and you were four inches taller.

The energy was palpable. Circles of friends assembled in assorted areas throughout the low-lit gym; half-dancing already, gossiping, hoping that "certain somebody" would be showing up that night, making lists of what songs you were going to request from Mr. DJ, and deciding what to do after the dance – going to Bob's Big Boy for shakes, or going to toilet paper some poor soul's house.

I remember my very first stake dance. My parents dropped me off outside the church, with a pep talk from my dad on how I should just grab the first girl I saw and use some pick-up line like, "Hey Sweetheart, teach me to dance." Apparently, my dad hadn't been 14 in many, many years. And "sweetheart" must have been a warmer salutation at that time, or on that planet.

I walked into that gym alone, the youngest guy in the room, and immediately scanned the place for any sign of safety or reassurance. I suddenly found it in the face of Sherri Rosquist, a friend from my Sunday school class. I hadn't been in the room two minutes and she came up to me.

"Hey, let's dance!" she said, grabbing my hand and pulling me with her. "I don't know how," I answered, as I walked out onto the floor with her. I really didn't feel timid about having never publicly danced before, as much as I felt I should legitimately warn her that things could get unsightly, if not physically and socially precarious for the both of us.

"I'll teach you," she kindly responded, with a big smile and all the confidence in the world.

Bless you, Sherri Rosquist. Bless you for saving me from a night of discomfiture and an entire adolescence of shame. Bless you for knowing how to dance. Bless you for your forwardness. And bless you for calling me back to the dance floor when, during the humming part near the end of Modern English's "I Melt with You," I assumed the song was over and started to exit from said dance floor.

As the song finally did end, I thanked Sherri and began walking away when a tall brunette stepped right in front of me and blocked my exit.

"Wanna dance?!" she beamed.

Oh, hold me. It was the spectacular Danielle Martin! She had been my regular babysitter when I was eight and she was twelve. And unless my memory is playing tricks on me, Danielle Martin looked precisely like Linda Carter, circa 1979.

I remembered Danielle well, as I'd had my suspicions when I was eight that Danielle may have had what scientists termed as "the hots" for me. After all, when the other kids were sent to bed, I was allowed to stay up and watch TV with her until we heard my parents pull into the driveway. At eight years old, that spelled out love to me! But our forbidden love had to be kept a secret.

But not anymore! Now I was 14 and she was a gorgeous 18-year-old, and we were on a dance floor! The scene was set, and all that we needed was the perfect soundtrack to celebrate the moment. So, you're probably thinking what I'm thinking. Yep. Cue the Hall & Oates.

The night continued down this magnificent path, enchanting moment after enchanting moment. I got jiggy wit it, I socialized with the "older" crowd, I delighted in the array of refreshments. It could not have been better.

And that's when I saw her.

She was beautiful, this nameless lady in a red dress, with dark hair and blue eyes. Of course, I can only assume you're thinking the same thing I'm thinking. Yep. Romance was in the air. Cue the Wham!

She was standing in the midst of several other attractive and significantly older women. 18-year olds. Well, thanks to a sensational experience earlier with Danielle Martin, plus an evening of flawless socializing … I was really overloaded with a false sense of confidence. I could not be shaken. I walked boldly up to Red Dress, completely convinced we would one day tell our grandchildren about this night.

"Wanna dance?" my voice warbled, surprising even myself.

It was the last song of the evening, and heaven bless her, she actually nodded her head. Wow. Really, the only thing that would have made the moment even better would have been if she'd instead just said, "Not a chance."

See, it quickly became evident that she hadn't done either of us any favors by agreeing to dance with me. She clearly didn't want to be there, and I clearly wanted her to be there so badly that my palms were sweating as if this dance were being judged by Church leaders themselves and my life hung in the balance.

Who was I to think an attractive 18-year-old woman was desperately waiting for a junior high kid to come make her evening by pulling her away from her ostentatious friends and out onto the dance floor in front of a condemnatory crowd to enjoy what had to have been the single longest love song ever recorded in the history of ever?

Not a word. Not a single word spoken between us. I blamed myself, of course. But I blamed her, too. Sure, I obviously put her in the difficult situation of not wanting to crush the spirit of an overly-zealous pubescent boy while also not wanting to dance with him … but once we found ourselves in this horrific predicament, she did absolutely nothing to save me. She didn't compliment me on my "Deacon Two-Step" (the quintessential dance move of all stake dance first-timers), she didn't ask if that was Drakkar Noir or Old Spice that I was wearing (it was both, I wanted to smell really special), and she didn't ask me what I thought of the intricate subtleties and underlying meanings behind Wham!'s "Careless Whisper," which was underscoring our unending dance. Nothing. Just complete, painful silence.

It felt like days had passed.

Finally, the song ended, our hands dropped to our sides, and we both did an about-face and marched away from each other, equally embarrassed and ashamed.

And that's life in a nutshell, my friends. Ups and downs. Peaks and valleys. Unstoppable, then humbled. Cloud Nine, then Cell Block Nine. But what a journey. And what a soundtrack! You're probably thinking what I'm thinking, right? Yep. Cue the Howard Jones.

Love at the Rocks

Written February 14, 2011

W ell, we're coming up on Valentine's Day, and love is in the air! Or in the toilet, I don't know. Frankly, I can't keep up with your love life.

Most of my Valentine's Day nostalgia takes place in elementary school, where we would gladly hand out Valentine's cards to everyone in class. Boy, girl, weird smelling kid with a lip fungus – everyone was endowed with a written sentiment. On Valentine's Day, charity abounded, and we were all compassionate. Then junior high happened and we were ashamed of ourselves for ever thinking that we could all be friends, especially with anybody not wearing Guess jeans. In high school, February 14th was pretty much just February 14th, and unless you were in love, love was not discussed. However, I do have some very specific Valentine's Day memories from my college era.

Valentine's Day, 1994. The scene: a wintery Provo, Utah. My love interest at the time, we'll call her Tamara (because that's her name), had only one Valentine's Day wish: that our special holiday dinner would take place at Olive Garden. Not a high-maintenance, gal, that Tamara;

evidenced by the fact she was willing to go out with me in the first place.

I called to make reservations but was informed by the college student de jour working the hostess desk that Olive Garden did not accept reservations. This should have alarmed me. But for some reason, the only inconvenient consequence I could fathom was that we would be sitting in the lobby of Olive Garden a smidge longer than we had originally thought; no big whoop.

There are questions of mortality that just can't be answered until the next life. What are the details or how matter was organized to create the earth? Why do some of our personal convictions conflict with scientific evidence? Why do bad things happen to good people? And why, in the face of all practicality, did I think I could simply show up at an extremely popular eatery on the evening of a nationally celebrated romantic holiday in a town that houses a university where dating is obligatory by decree ... and think that I would need to merely wait an extra five minutes for a table, and all would be well with the world?

We pulled up to Olive Garden, and it was complete anarchy. Hungry, frustrated crowds without reservations spilled out of the restaurant and into the parking lot, turning on each other. Women openly wept, men used language like "fetchin'" and "flippin'" as they paced around their cars ... outrageous! It was clear we were only moments away from someone exhibiting behavior usually reserved for Church basketball games.

I popped the car in reverse, looked over my shoulder, and did my best stuntman driving as we narrowly escaped the parking lot – couples and even restaurant employees jumping on my car, yelling at us, "Are you going to eat somewhere else?! Take us with youuuu!"

I explained to Tamara that we would simply jump on the I-15 and head north until we came across the next Olive Garden, somewhere between Provo and Salt Lake. She seemed on board, but 40 minutes later – with horrible traffic, icy weather, and our starving stomachs now digesting our livers – we decided we would just settle on the next restaurant we spotted.

And that's when it hit me.

Porter's Place.

Porter's Place (as described on their website) is a little, out-of-the-way restaurant located in Lehi on historic Main Street, in a 1915 brick building. And as the name suggests, it's dedicated to honoring Latter-day Saint Pioneer Orrin Porter Rockwell. Porter served as Joseph Smith's and Brigham Young's bodyguard and was one of the first converts to The Church of Jesus Christ. He was a close, personal friend of Joseph Smith, known for being a bit rough around the edges.

Now, if this doesn't scream Valentine's Day...I really don't know what does. Really.

I can't remember how I'd heard about the place, but I had a hunch that you did not need a reservation, and it would not be crowded. And sure enough, we sat right down. Imagine my delight to see that all the dishes were named after historical Latter-day Saint people and places. I enjoyed a delectable Parley P. Pratt (French dip pastrami with Swiss cheese) and Tamara had the Orson Hyde (a BLT). I was tempted by The Destroying Angel (a one-pound burger) but decided not to go to the dark side.

Having completely impressed Tamara by taking her to a romantic dinner at what was essentially a saloon, we decided to head back to my apartment for dessert and a video. (I know. HOW did she ever let me slip through her fingers?)

We were hummin' along the I-15 back to Provo when my car decided to no longer be a part of our plans, and … just … stopped. I pulled over and tried to start it again, but it was pouting and would not cooperate. I zipped up my jacket and jumped out of the car to wave down some help. Nuthin'. Car after car after car sped right on by, its occupants probably stuffed with Olive Garden and romantical thoughts, without a care in the world. Evidently brotherly love takes a holiday around Valentine's Day.

I jumped back in the car to warm up.

"Here's the thing," I said to Tamara. "I don't think anyone will stop for a strange man on the freeway in the middle of the night, in the middle of winter, this close to the state prison."

"Agreed," she smiled, not expecting my next sentence.

"And that's why I think if you get out, somebody will pull over right away. People will be quicker to help a young lady in distress."

She approved. At least, verbally.

Romantically, I opened her door for her and helped her out. (And they say chivalry is dead!) Then I watched her, and any chance of a good-night kiss, start walking away. Immediately, a car pulled over. My plan worked, but I still somewhat expected her to just get inside the guy's car and ride off with him, leaving me in the rain with my decrepit vehicle and a half-eaten Parley P. Pratt. I wouldn't have blamed her. But instead, he backed up, gave us a jump start, and away we went, before my alternator decided to go on strike again.

Back at my apartment, we dried off, warmed up, had dessert, and borrowed my roommate's functioning car so I could take Tamara home.

And you know what? Maybe it was because earlier in the day I had filled Tamara's room with red, pink, and white balloons. Maybe it was because she recognized it wasn't my fault that the Olive Garden didn't take reservations. Maybe it was because we spent the night laughing despite the escalating ridiculousness of the evening's events. But whatever the reasons, the night was highly entertaining, even if the date did not end predictably.

~

My Back in a Saddle Again

Written May 2, 2012

You've heard me tell the story about how I almost died at our stake Youth Conference because a pack of negligent teenagers dropped me during a "faith fall" object lesson, right? Out of a tree? 1988?

Well, that special event in my life has resulted in some creative methods for treating back pain over the years. Since 1988, I have undergone treatment from a series of chiropractors. Now, I am aware that there exists some skepticism surrounding this industry, but I have personally found success and relief through chiropractic care. There isn't that much controversy to me. I hurt, I get treated, I feel better.

However, like any profession, not all chiropractors are created equal.

Case in point: Dr. Arthur Fonzerelli. (Names have been changed.) (Because I can't remember his name.) Dr. Fonzerelli was probably in his late 50s, and when it came to his nose, he had a bit of an Ichabod Crane thing going on. He had thin hair on top, but it was still black.

Dr. Fonzi was the uncle of a girl I was dating in college, and his office happened to be in a neighboring town to our little university. It was

1993, and my back had recently been misbehaving. I was complaining about it to Danielle, the girl I was dating (name has not been changed, because I remember her name), and she suggested I go see her uncle, The Fonz. During this same time period I was also complaining that Sally Field was completely miscast as Robin William's wife in *Mrs. Doubtfire*, but Danielle said there was nothing she could do about that. Nice attitude. I believe that is what later led to our breakup.

Anyway, though initially reluctant, I finally paid a visit to the Doc, and surrendered a piece of my dignity that I can never retrieve. I visited his office exactly three times, and each appointment was more bizarre and unsettling than the one before.

First visit. He asked a lot of questions, gathered information, and took some x-rays. He did a pretty flaccid adjustment (I'm not sure that's the correct industry term for it) that was fairly benign, then told me I could leave. Not an efficacious treatment, but harmless enough. He was so soft spoken and uncle-y, I just kind of went with the flow and lowered my expectations of actually feeling better while simultaneously taking comfort in the fact that Danielle would be happy with me for being obedient and doing what she told me to do, and maybe I would be rewarded with some smooching. (But probably not.)

Second visit. At the beginning of the visit he said, "So, would you say there's been about 20% improvement since your last visit?" I started laughing, because I thought he was making a funny. I removed my shirt and turned to find him standing there with his clip board, pencil poised to write down my answer. He was serious. Not wanting him to feel bad, but feeling no different than before the first visit, I pretended to contemplate my percentage of wellness and kind of mumbled back,

"Erm…. uh…. Hmmhmm … two … (waving my hand back and forth) … maybe … I'd say two … percent … better?" He wrote it down.

"I think we're going to try something more aggressive," he said. "Like, addressing my back pain?" I wanted to ask. He led me into an adjoining room and had me sit/hunch forward over a bench, while he strapped some electrodes onto my lower back.

"We're going to try electrotherapy," he casually said.

"Okay," I responded with some trepidation.

"You're going to feel some currents through your back. It's going to be uncomfortable. I'm going to turn up the intensity with this dial, and you tell me when you can't stand it anymore."

"TIME OUT," I said. "I don't like to play games like this."

"You'll be just fine," and he started to turn it up.

I tried to be my bravest for as long as I could. "Mercy!" I said.

"Okay," he answered. "I'm going to leave it there for 10 minutes."

"What the WHAT?!"

And he left the room. I had never felt this variation of pain before, and it was intense! I felt like something was alive and kicking in me, and I was going to give birth to it – through my CHEST! Currents were having a rave inside my body and I could only anticipate death and my corpse detonating, leaving parts of me covering the entire room. The good news is, if I am ever hit by lightning, it'll be a walk in the park.

And imagine my surprise, when I actually *did* feel better when he turned the machine off! Kind of like how your face feels better once somebody stops hitting it with a car. Or how silence sounds so nice when Nickleback is the alternative. I went home, exhausted and confused.

Third and final visit. I walked into his office, and he asked me to strip down to what the Fashion World terms "tighty-whities." Not totally unusual; easy access to my back and all. He asked me again, "Where would you say, percentage-wise, your improvement is at? 20%?"

I stood there with the same incredulous expression as the visit before, but this time, much more vulnerable, as I looked like I was an underwear model. Well, I looked like I was *modeling* underwear. (I've never, on my best day, looked like an underwear *model*.) I mumbled the same response as the prior visit. "Wha-? … uhrm … yeeeaahhh … two … (waving my hand back and forth) ... maybe … I'd say two percent?"

"We're going to try something different today (oh, good!), so…follow me."

My relief was short lived, as I started following him from our private patient room … out the door … into the hallway. I found myself standing in the public domain, with only my underwear on. I could see the waiting room. And they could see me. Like one of those dreams. But despite the ethereal music of Enya that permeated the office, this was indeed no dream.

If you were sitting in the right (or wrong) spot in the waiting room, you had a comprehensive view of more Ken Craig than most people care to see. I've never seen more raised eyebrows in my life, as people shook their heads, covered children's eyes, and kept a careful distance between them and me.

We stopped in the middle of the hallway, at some adjusting apparatus there. Yes! In the middle of the hallway! Did somebody leave it there accidentally? Was this really the best place for this thing?

"Go ahead and lie down on this," he said.

And, as if under some form of hypnosis, I did what he asked. No sooner was I horizontal, but clamps snapped over my wrists and ankles, strapping me to the table and rendering me unable to stand back up, get off the table, and flee from his office out into the streets; cold and exposed, but safe.

He pulled a lever and the table jolted into a vertical position. Now I was standing, in my skivvies, strapped to a table. This equipment could not have been legal. I'm not even sure it was 20th century machinery. Then, the straw that broke me: Dr. Fonz put his hand on my lower back and started rapidly pushing my torso forward. Push, release. Push, release. I suddenly looked like I was doing my best Elvis impression. In my underwear. In the hallway. In a torture device.

That was it for me.

I started talking very fast, in a half-panicked voice, like a kid trying to sell a lie to his parents. "Yep. Yep, I'd say I can definitely feel a twenty percent improvement. Twenty or maybe even 25!"

Push, release. Push, release.

"What did Danielle say to you? Did she tell you I didn't like *Mrs. Doubtfire*? Did that personally offend you?"

Push, release. Push, release.

Finally, after what felt like 18 years, he stopped, unstrapped me, and we went back to his office. I put my clothes on while he filled out paperwork. He then said, "I'm not sure what else will help you." He seemed so defeated. I almost felt bad for him. I probably would have continued to see him just to make him feel better, except that his practices terrified me. Who knows what he would have tried next?! "If you jump out of this plane without a parachute, I really think the landing will give you a twenty percent improvement. Here, hand me your pants before you jump ..."

You'd think this single experience would have steered me clear of chiropractic doctors, but the truth is I've had exceptional care from the chiropractors I've met since then. The only real fallout from my adventure with Dr. Fonza-crazy-pants is that to this day, I can't listen to Enya without instinctively and subconsciously dancing like Elvis. And I have no tolerance for *Mrs Doubtfire*, but that was a pre-existing condition.

IN THE MOOD FOR FOOD

"First we eat, then we do everything else."

– M.F.K. Fisher

Delicious McCandy

Written December 13, 2005

If you and I are going to be friends, there is something you should know about me. I am, hands down, the biggest sucker for new things. This applies to a number of areas of interest, really, but I am specifically intrigued by new *food*.

Many are the moments I am standing in line at the grocery store when I notice a new confection that almost causes me to have a hernia right there in the express lane. Have you noticed over the last year or so that the candy bar industry has taken a very real interest in launching variations on their already existing delectables? Words fail me in expressing the joy that has entered my life from the delights of White Chocolate Reese's Peanut Butter Cups, Mint Kit Kats, Cherry Chocolate Kisses and Chocolate Peppermint Patties.

And I am a helpless pawn in the candy bar game, because I will fall for whatever they put in front of me that looks new. If I were standing in line at the store and I saw a new Hershey bar called "Chocorubbernougat: milk chocolate, creamy nougat, and burnt rubber tires" my eyes would bug out, I would snatch it up with great fervor, and I would think to myself "Wow! Nougat AND burnt rubber?! HOW has nobody thought of this BEFORE?! Sure, I wouldn't eat a car tire on its own, but *with* chocolate *and* nougat, it *must* be delicious!" And then I would buy two of them.

Even more shocking is my sudden interest in the McRib, back for a limited time only. McDonald's McRib sandwich, while not technically new, is a "food" that I have had in my peripheral vision since I was a child, yet have never tried.

When I was young and impressionable I was convinced it had to be the ultimate food stuff. I mean … ribs! Ribs *and* French fries! C'mon!

But I grew up in southern California, where In-N-Out reigned supreme as the reason hamburgers were even invented, so there was never a reason to frequent McDonalds. And now, with my own family, we also patronize our local In-N-Out.

In fact, if there was a national award for The American Family Most Unfamiliar with McDonalds, the Craig family would win in a landslide. In truth, our only experience with McDonalds was on a road trip some years back, when it was the only place available to grab some "food." Each of my children got sick from this one, single McDonald's experience. Two years later, and they *still* remember it well. Just last week my son Connor wasn't feeling great. When I asked him how he was doing he said, "I feel like I went to McDonalds and *accidentally* ate a hamburger." "Like you ate a Big Mac?" I asked. "A WHAT Mac?" he answered.

Katie's feelings towards McDonalds became crystal clear to me the other night when, after a commercial, I mentioned I was thinking of going there for lunch the next day and trying a McRib. "What?! You might as well go to a strip club!" she said.

I assumed she was being facetious, so went anyway. (To McDonalds, not the strip club.) I was almost giddy with the anticipation of eating my very special rib sandwich, a meal 25 years in the making. I went to lunch by myself that day, as it felt like something I should do alone. Like going to the bathroom or listening to Wham! I went through the drive-thru and placed my order.

"Medium Fries and a McRib, please."

"Would you like to try an Eggnog shake today?"

A WHAT-nog? Could this be a *new* shake, available *for a limited time only*? Oh, sister, I pray you aren't toying with me. It's like she knew about my weakness. "WOULD I!" I answered. A McRib sandwich and an Eggnog shake! This was going to be the best lunch ever!

I found the nearest empty parking lot and pulled over, directly. I removed the McRib goodness from the cardboard container and marveled at how messy it looked. I sunk my teeth into the McStuff and … and … I was pretty much *under*whelmed. I mean, it was exactly how you would imagine it to taste. Maybe there was too much pressure for it to really measure up. Maybe I was expecting too much from McDonalds. Or maybe…just MAYBE…if you combined the McRib with burnt rubber tire! Mmm…the McRubberRib. It *has* to be good!

Love in the Time of Lemon Zinger

Written May 19, 2011

I f by chance you've had the opportunity to view the John Cusack/ Kate Beckinsale movie *Serendipity*, then you'll remember the be- ginning of the movie and you don't have to read the rest of this paragraph. If not, drop everything, come over right now, and I'll show it to you so you understand the rest of my story. Or just read this brief synopsis: at the end of their serendipitous meeting, Ms. Beckinsale writes her name and phone number on the inside cover of the book *Love in the Time of Cholera* and tells John Cusack that the next morn- ing she is going to sell it to a used book store. If he finds it, then fate will bring them back together. Fast-forward years and years and see Mr. Cusack as each time he passes a used bookstore, he picks up *Love in the Time of Cholera* and looks inside for that phone number.

For years and years.

Dear John Cusack, I get it. I have been on such a quest.

It was summer, 2002. Avril Lavigne was demanding to know why we had to go and make things so comp-li-cated and Leonardo DiCap- rio was taunting us to catch him if we could. And most importantly,

I walked into an Albertson's one afternoon and unsuspectingly picked up a carton of Blue Bunny Ice Cream's limited-edition flavor ... Lemon Zinger. And my life was never again the same.

Lemon Zinger was a concoction of lemon ice cream, vanilla wafer chunks, and delicate lemon truffles – all swirled together with lemon meringue. We ate it exclusively all summer.

And then it disappeared.

Yes, Blue Bunny had warned us that it was a "limited edition," but I refused to believe it. I thought it was a "limited edition" the way that the Las Vegas Athletic Club has a "limited time $5 enrollment." (That "limited time" has been running the entire 13 years I've lived in Las Vegas.)

Fast-forward years and years. It is now 2011. For nine years, each time I have entered a grocery store, I have walked the ice cream aisle, hoping against hope to find Lemon Zinger on the shelf. Not once.

Have other flavors come into my life? Oh, heavens, yes. Are they superior to Lemon Zinger? Most likely. But how could I know? To not be able to have it – that is what pains me. It became my crutch. "I'm sorry I'm being so cranky today – I haven't had Lemon Zinger in 8 years." "I would do the dishes, but it throws me into bouts of depression since none of the dishes are dirtied with Lemon Zinger."

It finally came to a head last January. For work, I happened to be at a grocer trade show, here in the L. V. Low n' behold, Blue Bunny had a booth. I approached. A Blue Bunny employee stepped up and smiled. "Can I help you with anything?" she asked.

Always the professional, I looked her directly in the eye. "Here's why I hate you," I started, and then began an emotional diatribe about my long-lost Lemon Zinger that had been festering in me for almost a decade. It ended in tears. She tried to console me with a Blue Bunny ice cream sandwich. Through my tears, I unwrapped it, held it in one hand and crushed it into my other palm, like putting out a cigar. I didn't even blink or look away, even though it was cold and stung a little. But I was enraged and had a point to make.

"I'm sorry," she said, motioning for security. "But there just wasn't enough of a demand for it."

"Not enough of a demand?" I loudly and indignantly barked. "Lady, let me tell you a little story about a TV show called *Seinfeld*. Perhaps you've heard of it? Then perhaps you're aware that the first season or two there was no demand for *Seinfeld*. Believe it! But NBC kept it around, giving it some time to catch on. Some time to be appreciated, recognized, and develop a following. And maybe – just MAYBE – it developed SUCH a demand that it became the most widely successful television show OF ALL TIME! How's THAT for a demand, sister?! Lemon Zinger could have become Blue Bunny's *Seinfeld*. But now … now, you'll never know. You blew it. I hope you can live with yourself. You disgust me."

I turned to walk away, but went back. "If you still have any of those ice cream sandwiches left, I'd like one, please. And I promise not to smash this one into my hand."

I share this experience now because about two weeks ago I stepped into a Baskin-Robbins to get a birthday surprise for a friend. The Baskin-Robbins lady was preparing my order and asked, "Would you like to try a sample of our Flavor of the Month?"

Well, I'm not the world's most passionate guy, but I'm not stupid either, so I said, "All right." She handed me a spoonful of what appeared to be ice cream, and I shoved it in my mouth.

It wasn't ice cream. It was heaven-churned heavenliness of frozen heaven. The taste came right back to me.

"What is this?!" I wept, and ran to the counter to read the label. Baskin Robbins Golden Oreo Gold Rush. Lemon custard ice cream and Oreo icing ribbon, topped with Golden Oreo cookie pieces.

Is it exactly the same? Not ingredient-for-ingredient. Does my mouth know the difference? No. No, it doesn't. Spoiler Alert: Mr. Cusack eventually found his book … and I … I have found my ice cream. I have been to Baskin Robbins several times since then. And I hope May never ends.

~

Unhealthy Statistics

Written May 9, 2008

From time to time I receive a bulky and unsolicited health magazine in my mailbox. I've never subscribed to it, and I've never paid for it. And in spite of its large print and vibrant pictures, I am still able to generally ignore it. But this time, as I walked home with nothing more to read from the mailbox but the power bill (and I like to be sitting down when I read that), I thumbed through the magazine. And you won't believe what I found: That's right – an article on colons!

Now, it's been my experience that this topic is among the top three No-No's in social conversations: Religion, Politics, and Colons. For example, this joke will never end well: "So the Pope, a Rabbi, and Bill Clinton walk into a bar, each with their own colon under one arm, and a bottle of Kaopectate under the other..."

But here are some startling statistics I found in this article.

In Their Lifetime, the Average American Eats...

6 whole Pigs

12 three-thousand-pound cows

3,000 chickens, turkeys, and other flying birds

3,000 fish, sea creatures and sea scavengers

2,000 gallons of alcohol

300 soft drinks

400 candy bars

500 doughnuts

It wasn't until the second time I read through these statistics that I realized the author of this article wasn't bragging about how awesome Americans are in eating contests or at killing things.

Now, I don't know where he gathered his information, but I see some real inaccurate calculations here. And I am going to now correct him, but without doing any additional research of my own. Because seriously, I've read that, like, 82% of statistics are made up anyway.

6 Whole Pigs: This may actually be correct. When you take into account the numerous delicious ways to eat pigs, I would be embarrassed to *not* eat 6 pigs during my lifetime. From sausage and bacon to Easter ham and pork chops, it's truly the other white meat. And when it says "whole" pigs, I assume it includes toenails, eyelashes, lips, ears, and spleen. And I think that is correct because hot dogs cover those areas. So, this could be the most accurate statement in this statistical analysis.

12 Three-thousand-pound cows: WRONG. How would you even know that? What if I just ate one huge 36,000-pound cow instead of 12 average-sized cows? Maybe I found it roaming elusively, undomesticated in the wild frontier of Wyoming somewhere? Are you suggesting it would be better to let such an animal run free, menacing the countryside and eating small Wyomian children? How un-American are YOU, pal?

3,000 Flying Birds: I can kind of see what he's saying here, and I tend to agree. This is really a suggestion that we branch out and try new things; namely, flightless birds. When was the last time you tried Ostrich? Or a delicious slice of Penguin? Come on people, get out of your comfort zones. Don't be afraid to try new things.

3,000 Sea Animals: I'll tell you right now that if he is including shrimp in this statistic, he is way low. I've eaten 3,000 shrimp in one sitting. (They are so tiny!) And if you go to Claim Jumper, (slogan: Gluttony! Successful Capitalism! Come see why the rest of the world hates America!), I'm pretty sure you can now order a surf n' turf combo of 3,000 shrimp with half of a pig. It's called the Swimming Swine. Top it off with an éclair the size of your head, and that is a fine, fine meal, my friend.

2,000 Gallons of Alcohol: If this is accurate, I am way, way behind. I've never even had heavy duty cough syrup.

300 Soft Drinks: I'm sorry, did this survey say "in a lifetime" or "before noon?" I know people in my office who take soda intravenously until lunchtime, so it is difficult to declare, within any degree of accuracy, just how much Diet Coke is coursing through them at any one time. If somebody has a soda once a day, then they've had 300 sodas before the end of one calendar year. There is no way this number is right. Unless this statistic is from 1948.

400 Candy Bars: If the 24-hour period after October 31 is considered a Free Zone and those numbers don't count towards the rest of the year, then I could see this being close to accurate.

500 Doughnuts: (Or as I like to call it, Appetizer Item #5 at Claim Jumper.) Difficult to say on this one. If you eat one with a fork and knife, is it still a doughnut, or is it now cake? If you take a dozen Krispy Kreme glazed donuts, put them in a bowl, pour milk over them, and call them Cheerios, are they still doughnuts, or are they now cereal? That sounds good … maybe I should do some real research and get back to you on that one.

Regardless if these statistics are accurate, I think we can all agree on one thing: when it comes to killing and eating things, you can bet that 78% of the time, Americans are the best at it 100% of the time.

Sugar-Free January

Written February 1, 2006

Me (Standing): Hi. My name is Ken Craig...and I'm addicted to sugar.

Rest of the world: Hi, Ken...

Me (Taking deep breath): Well, I suppose it all started this past holiday season ...

We as a society have embraced the reality that from the last week of November through the end of the year is pretty much a food fest, right? Well, for some wonderful reason, Food Fest 2005 was easily the most abundantly delectable year *ever* for our household. It was plate after plate after plate after plate after plate after plate of sweet, sugary, chocolaty, fudgy, bread-y, gooey goodness. It was magical. Generous friends and neighbors after generous friends and neighbors dropping off treats like clockwork. It actually became labor intensive to try and finish it all off. It was like we were spending the holidays at Willy Wonka's factory. No, it was like we had moved to the town of Chewandswallow in the book *Cloudy with a Chance of Meatballs* and the weatherman predicted 'sweets.'

I loved every delicious, fattening moment of it.

Then, one night at dinner, Katie had an idea. An awful idea! My wife had a wonderful, awful idea!

"You know," she said, carving a slice of dinner-cake for herself, "We've really been eating a lot of sugar this month."

"I'll say!" I chimed in, serving myself seconds of the fresh fudge and toffee and topping off my Eggnog. "It's glorious, isn't it kids!"

"Oh, yes, Father!" they agreed, pouring dressing on their tossed lemon bars. "Is this what they mean by Christmas Spirit?"

"*This is it!*" I validated, taking a napkin and wiping some kind of glucose-generated froth off my youngest daughter's mouth.

"Well," Katie spoke up, "I was thinking that since December has been our month of sugar, maybe January could be our month of NO sugar."

We all froze, perfectly still. Just kidding. Of course there was way too much sugar coursing through any of us to actually be "still," but it definitely got quieter. Then the kids spoke up, led by my eager-to-please daughter, Abbie, "That's a great idea, Mom!"

"Are you INSANE!?" I thought to myself. "How could a person actually cut out sugar? And WHY – for the love of heaven, WHY?!"

I mean, in theory I agreed with Katie. And when I say "in theory," what I mean is that I didn't really agree with her at all. What she was essentially saying was, "Since December was a month of happiness, how about January be a month of NO happiness?"

But after we put the kids in bed to enjoy their sugar-induced comas, Katie and I got out some hot chocolate and pumpkin pie, sat on the couch, and discussed the idea some more. For the sake of side-stepping an enormous dental bill, we decided to take a stab at it. And on December 31st, we put all items containing sugar in the trash. In actuality, I thought it was a pretty good idea.

Around noon on January 1st, I thought it was a horrible idea. My body wanted sugar like Jim Carrey wants an Academy Award.

Now, giving up sugar during the day is one thing. But my nights, though … oh, my nights. It's tradition for Katie and me to enjoy a treat together regularly at night when we are unwinding. That wasn't just a December thing – *that's a ten years of marriage thing!* So at night, when we'd be sitting watching TV or reading or something, I was craving sweets something fierce. Often were the nights I would casually announce that I was going to the kitchen to get a drink of sugar-free tap water, but once there, I would frantically tear that kitchen apart as if I could smell sugar coming from somewhere.

Start with the freezer. Hmm … frozen corn! Aw, it's not even Sweet Corn! Next, the fridge. Hey – cheese! Does cheese have sugar? It's dairy – same family as ice cream. Maybe a cold bowl of cheese! No. Then, the pantry. Come on, come on … there's got to be something sugary in here. Hello, what's this in the back … behind the cooking oil – hey, cooking oil? Nah – But what is this back here … it's … it's … oh, hold me; it's a single, old packet of Nestle hot chocolate, long since forgotten. It's a New Year's miracle!

I decided that, in an effort to help me make it through the first few weeks of this Sugar-Free January nonsense, I should chronicle the experiment in a daily log. I was going to call it a Sugar Log, but that just sounded too delicious, and I was distracted every time I went to write something down; not to mention I drooled excessively on the pages of the book and it became too sticky to write on them. So instead, I just titled it *My Descent into Madness: The Autobiography of Ken Craig's January.*

January 1: 9:00 a.m. Woke up feeling fantastic. Enjoyed an egg and toast for breakfast. Actually, kind of looking forward to the detoxification and purging sugar from my body. A new healthier, happier me.

January 1: 9:15 a.m. Ransacked house looking for sugar. Checked pantry, fridge, 72-hour kits – even searched hard-to-reach areas for possible overlooked plastic eggs filed with Easter candy from 9 months ago.

January 4: Wept. Like a baby. Felt moody all day. Punished one of my children for "not being funny enough at the dinner table" and sent him to bed. Lethargic. Unshaven. Kicked the dog.

January 5: Realized I don't own a dog. Wrote apology note to neighbors for kicking their dog. Tied note to brick and threw it through their window.

January 6: Ate entire jar of Sweet Pickles. Contacted lawyer for "false advertising" claim. Wondering where I can locate some Sugar Beets.

January 9: Promised Katie the Sugar Nazi that if she let me eat a bowl of ice cream I'd watch *Project Runway* with her. Nothing doin'.

January 10: Promised Katie if I could eat a package of Hostess Donuts I'd look at the IKEA catalogue with her and pretend we lived in Manhattan and had a 600 square foot apartment. Nope.

January 11: Suggested we celebrate our 11 days of "Sugar Free January" success with celebratory cake and ice cream! One cake per person! Vetoed.

January 12: Packed a hobo sack, flung it over my shoulder, started whistling "Pour Some Sugar on Me," and told Katie I was hitchhiking to The Big Rock Candy Mountain. She tried to convince me there was no such place. (As if I'm going to fall for that Sugar Nazi propaganda!)

January 14: Came back home, listless. I think my body is imploding. Bones weakening. Organs leaking vital fluids. Heart slowing. Breathing shallow. Darkness closing in. Slight headache.

January 15: While hallucinating, tried to eat plastic cupcake in daugh-ter's toy kitchen. Once hallucinations stopped, tried once more to eat cupcake. Found bag of Ruffles potato chips instead. Ate entire bag. And also the chips.

January 16: Realized this is just going to be one long month of zero happiness. Katie told me to pour myself a big heaping bowl of "Shut the Heck Up". Poured myself a bowl of raisins instead. That's what happens when you're living under a Sugar Nazi regime!

KIDS THESE DAYS

"Two roads diverged in the wood, and

I –

I took the one less tweeted about."

UR TXTNG 2 MUCH

Written August 4, 2010

In case you weren't sure where I stood on such key principles, I'm really not one of those dads who feels that his kids watching a DVD on a road trip is ruining "Family Time." Today's world offers such amenities, and that's fine. Of course, this isn't the same world that I grew up in. If it were, my kids would be unbuckled, lying down in the back of the Family Van, going to wherever, sharing the space with six siblings, listening to *Unforgettable Fire* on their Walkman while they "rewound" their *Listen Like Thieves* cassette tape by sticking a pen in the spokes of the tape and whirling it around in order to rewind it by hand, thus saving the batteries in the Walkman for strictly playing cassette tapes, rather than rewinding them. (And yes, in the next life, when the pioneers try to tell me how rough they had it, I am planning on bringing up this hardship in my defense.)

In short, I'm not your middle-aged fuddy-duddy neighbor who poo-poos all technological advances and thinks they are the demise of our children's' character. On the whole, I actually embrace such advances. However, I do have my limits.

Recently I had the unanticipated opportunity to put my head in my hands, angry and appalled, and weep at the thought of our future world leaders. It began innocently enough; I was summoned to listen to a co-worker weave a tale of her daughter's first date with this "super-cute" boy. (I cannot emphasize those quotation marks enough.)

"So," the female co-worker begins, "they were sitting in the movie, and about 10 minutes into the movie he texts her!"

"Wait," I interrupted. "Were they sitting next to each other?"

"Yes!" she said, not detecting my disdain, "and do you know what he texted? He texted, 'Can I hold your hand?'"

"AAAAAAAAAHHHHOOOOOHHHHHHHH!" cooed all the women in the office.

I stood there, stone-faced. I did not coo. I did not cheer. But I had the restraint to not say what I wanted to say, which was, "THAT IS TO-TALLY CHEATING!"

I'm sorry, but that is not how the game is played. I understand how the power of texting provides a false sense of bravado and you can say (or ask) things you would never in a ba-jillion years do otherwise. And I can see the allure of going that route. I mean, I've wanted to quit jobs, inform somebody their fly was down, and tell off my waitress all through the power of texting, rather than the more direct and tradi-tional manner of talking face-to-face.

But brother, you are not doing yourself any favors by skipping the en-tire dance that is hand-holding. You are missing the joy and satisfac-tion of one of life's greatest accomplishments. The patience, the read-ing of body language, the nuances and subtleties of movements, the wishing, the hoping, the fear, the anxiety, the pit in your stomach, the palm-sweats, the glances, the skin brushing. And when those fingers finally lock, it has all been worth it. You can almost hear angels singing.

As an authority on the art of hand-holding, with mucho know-how and enough experience to write a ~~book~~ brief pamphlet on the subject, allow me to walk you through what the experience would have been, won't you?

Where were we, ten minutes into the movie? That's not when you text to see if you can hold the girl's hand; that is when you are wondering if she is going to be appalled at the amount of popcorn you can eat in one sitting.

15 Minutes: You observe the boundaries. What are the physical obstacles between you and her? A bucket of popcorn? Sodas? Her purse? A wall of anticipation so thick you have to poke it to measure the density?

30 Minutes: You lean towards her, possibly brushing shoulders. First contact. You realize you are paying very little attention to anything going on in the movie at this point.

45 Minutes: You casually place your arm on the armrest of the chair, and slyly look out of the side of your eye to see if she has done likewise. You leave it there for 20 minutes to give her ample opportunity to A) notice it, B) appreciate the opportunity to eat some of the popcorn that you are no longer inhaling, and C) casually move her own arm in that direction. Hands now in the same proximity.

60 Minutes: What the WHAT?! Your hands were so close, and now she has just as casually put her hands in her lap! You do the same, not wanting to appear desperate.

70 Minutes: Hands are inconspicuously back in proximity of each other. You've observed and retained about 15 minutes of the entire movie so far, completely preoccupied now by how dangerously close you are to lightly brushing up against her hand with yours – just to see what kind of reflex you get from her. Then you make the move – hand sweeps past hers, lightly touching. Does her hand move? Does it begin to take the direction of opening, fingers prepared to go inter-digitary with yours? Does it completely sit still? Does it actually recoil, going back into her lap, with her saying, "Oh, sorry," assuming you accidentally bumped her? You both retreat, hands back to yourselves.

75 Minutes: The side of your pinky is now flat up against hers on the armrests. There's contact, and nobody is withdrawing. You lift your pinky slightly, and her hand begins to slide into your now-shared space. It's happening! Your hand slides over the top of her hand, she slides under yours, and your hands both turn and CLASP!

Euphoria!

Somewhere, the Hallelujah chorus is being belted out. To the on-looking movie goers, nothing has really changed, but internally, you are a volcano of emotions! You go temporarily deaf and can't hear anything going on in the movie, your heart is visibly pounding in your chest, and your hand immediately begins to sweat, but you don't dare break away and wipe it on your jeans. It might break the spell!

In fact, you consciously avoid any movement of your entire appendage whatsoever. You don't want to draw too much attention to your date that you are, in fact, holding hands and probably going to get married someday. You are now a team as you watch this movie. You laugh at the same parts, even making comments to each other (which up to this point had been taboo).

90 Minutes. You remember nothing of the movie – other than it was your favorite movie EVER because you got to hold hands with your date!

Give all that up for the ease of a text message? I think not. Don't surrender life's delightful nuances to the crassness of technology. Please, join me in being a responsible tech-user.

(However, that being said; if my fly is down, as an act of goodwill, please consider texting me about it, rather than discussing it. That's the kind of awkwardness we can all sidestep with the appropriate use of technology.)

~

Non-Incriminating Evidence

Written January 28, 2013

Sometimes when I really want to freak out the youth at church I tell them about when Sister Craig and I were dating, back in 1995. I weave tales about how I would sometimes, unannounced, just pop in at her apartment. And how sometimes…she wouldn't be there! AND I WOULD HAVE NO IDEA WHERE SHE WAS OR WHEN SHE WAS COMING BACK! I would have to do something crazy like LEAVE A HANDWRITTEN NOTE, TELLING HER TO CALL ME LATER! And then sometime, later that day, she'd hopefully get that note and call me. And MAYBE I would be at my apartment to answer my land-line phone, and MAYBE I WOULDN'T! Maybe I'd be out, and I actually wouldn't have any communication with her that entire afternoon or even that day! No communication! Like we were animals! And can you even stand the suspense of when we would see each other again?! I know!

Seriously, I sound ancient to these youth when I tell stories of living before every soul had a cell phone with texting or Find a Friend capabilities. And you know what? I totally feel archaic, too! I find my own self sitting there in a daze wondering how we lived so crippled by our lack of technology. I swear in 1995 it was like we had evolved one measly step from chimps playing with sticks. "And then to show Sister Craig I was interested in her romantically, I thumped my chest and handed her a branch that was on fire. She prayed about it, and we got married."

Doesn't it feel as if society has so quickly adapted to all of us being absolutely accessible at all times, we can't fathom a time when it wasn't that way? You may even find yourself thinking back on moments when you would have saved time, resources, and emotional anguish if we were all using Smart Phones and texting and apps. I've done that.

But the upside is this, my ancient friend, you also lived out your pubescent years at a time when the entire world didn't have video camera/phones on their person 24 hours a day; and then a medium to immediately distribute that video to the public.

I mean, of course we were never 100% sure how awesome anything we did was because we couldn't film it and immediately broadcast it to be validated by the public … but for those of us who are products from the 70s, 80s, or 90s … I think we are actually grateful for that. I know I am.

My family bought a home video camera in 1984. I was 13. THIRTEEN! The only wise decision I ever made in my adolescent awkwardness (besides keeping my crush on Olivia Newton-John a secret) was to completely avoid being on camera. Sure, it was a fascinating new technology, but I knew better. In fact, the only two documented video sightings of me as a teenager is one of me yelling at my cousin to stop videotaping me, and the other is of me at age 16, at a ward Roadshow practice. And people, believe me, it is obnoxious! Probably because I was obnoxious at 16! I am on stage chewing a piece of gum like I'm doing it a favor and providing more eye rolls than legally allowed by the FCC.

Think on your own teen years and imagine being surrounded by friends who are constantly prepared to video whatever foolishness you are prone to! Here's a list of what you and I were spared by me being a teen of the 80s and as a result, no rogue video floating around:

*I played water polo. Nobody needs to see what that looked like. (This was before the "hip," less-offensive Speedos you see in the Summer Olympics now.)

*Once during my sophomore year of high school, I had to go up to the board to diagram a sentence in my English class. My pants caught on a broken part of a desk as I walked to the front and ripped a hole on the area of my jeans covering my bum. Not cool. It was a YouTube moment waiting to happen … but mercifully, there was no YouTube!

*My first kiss was at a Youth Conference, on a bus, in front of millions of people. Whew, dodged a bullet there.

*My freshman year I played the clarinet. In the marching band. At football games. Nobody beat me up or gave me a wedgie, but they should have. And that would have been on Facebook for sure. (There wasn't the anti-bullying movement that you see nowadays. I guess it was an era when people figured if you were in the marching band then you had it coming. And it's hard to argue with that logic.)

Home: Where My Wall Is Your Canvas

Written March 20, 2012

I'm not always the trendsetter in the crowd, so I'm not super clear on when vinyl lettering became The Thing that Everybody Should Be Doing.

You know the ones; you see them on the walls of living rooms everywhere. "All Because Two People Had to Get Married" or "Netflix: The Center of Our Home."

I'm going to admit right here and now that we don't have any up in our house. So, we're obviously in the market. But HOW does one decide which platitude or adage to go with?

Life is not measured by the breaths we take

but by the moments that take our breath away.

Doctrinally speaking, I'm actually not sure either of these measurements will be brought up on The Final Exam. I'm picturing Angels reviewing your Book of Life. "Looks like your breath was only taken away twice. TWICE! This doesn't bode well for you. I'm just telling you that now, so you're not surprised or disappointed later."

Live well, laugh often, love much.

Too bossy.

Make each day your masterpiece.

Too much pressure.

The laundry room. Loads of fun.

False advertising.

The best and most beautiful things in the world

cannot be seen or even touched.

They must be felt with the heart.

As well as written in fancy calligraphy.

A girl should be two things; classy and fabulous.

I think this one is from the new *For the Strength of Youth* pamphlet.

So, I'm open to suggestions. Stop by anytime. My living room wall is your canvas!

The Birds, The Bees &
The Guinea Pigs

Written June 28, 2006

I don't maintain a Bucket List, but if I did, "Own a Guinea Pig" would not make the cut, and "Breed Guinea Pigs" would be on a different list, altogether, like the "I Would Sooner Kick the Bucket Than Do This" list. But in some of those Life's Great Lessons, your life happens to be the punch-line. Nowhere is this truer than in parenting.

Before you and your spouse ever ring that bell that can't be un-rung, round that corner that can't be un-rounded, or empty that toothpaste tube that can't be…er…you know…stuffed back up with toothpaste, nobody can completely, comprehensively explain to you how your brain will never be the same. Or, how you'll be too tired or too in love to really even care.

In populating the planet, you are producing replicants who will do unspeakable things to your shirt while you lovingly swaddle them as infants. Then you will catch them doing impressions of you for their friends during the adolescent years. And finally, they will ignore your savvy, unsolicited advice as young adults. Yet your addled brain will always see them as delightful children who won your heart from their very first breath.

Before I had kids, I would have openly mocked any parent who suggested to my face that I would alter my lifestyle in any way after having children of my very own. "Watch *Sleeping Beauty* at my daughter's request when there's a *Seinfeld* rerun on? Oh, no," I would retort, putting a brick in my glove and smacking the pride out of their face, "I demand satisfaction. I will not be changing the selfish standard of living I have established for myself."

And then it happened. I had kids, and I morphed into some kind of reputable, lovesick idiot. I suppose I owe all those soothsayer-parents who foretold my behavior an apology. But they aren't going to get one.

I now live an existence rich with events and acts that were once inconceivable to me. Have you ever been miles from the nearest rest-stop, squatting outside your mini-van in the rain, holding your four-year old in the air by the sides of his bum so he can "unburden" himself outside the vehicle, to the delight of passing semi-trucks? Ever had your child inform your ecclesiastical leader, "It's a good thing you stopped by our home right now. Usually after 9 p.m. my dad just walks around in his underwear!"? In the name of heaven, have you ever looked into your child's eyes and seen the horror in their soul as they realize they are going to be in trouble for taking more than they could eat, so to save them, you finish their bowl of wet, soggy Lucky Charms? The humanity! But I do it. For the love of my brood, I perform acts of service that I simply do not expect non-parents to understand.

Case in point: Recently, my daughter Abbie decided that her guinea pig, TJ, should have babies. You know, to pass on the TJ family name. To grow her posterity. To leave a legacy during her lifetime.

I don't have any proof, but my impression is that TJ is probably more interested in having babies because she is going to need someone to take care of her when she's old. Last I checked, she had paid virtually nothing into her 401K and IRA accounts. Also, most of her life has been spent working part-time gigs as a cage fighter and getting paid under the table, so she won't qualify for Social Security either.

Essentially, her children would be her retirement fund, and if she doesn't get busy, she's going to end up childless and in Guinea Pig Hospice.

Abbie assured me we would not have to keep all the guinea pig babies, so I relented and agreed to pimp TJ out to the most qualified male guinea pig in the tri-state area. Abbie had recently been to the birthday party of a friend who received, as one of her presents, a male guinea pig. Coincidence? I think not.

So, in one of the most awkward phone conversations on record, we invited this family over one Saturday night, and requested they bring Chuck, their guinea pig, to enjoy a romp on our stud farm. It was all under the guise of Enjoying Dessert Together, but essentially, it was so our guinea pigs could get it on (to coin a phrase). And I don't care where you're from, that's weird.

On top of the weirdness was a generous helping of novel emotions on my part. I was suddenly suspicious of Chuck. What kind of guinea pig was he? What was his upbringing? What kind of education did he have? How was he going to provide for this new family of his? If he was like the other guinea pigs I'd met, I could tell you how he was going to provide for them – he wasn't! And then I'd have all these little fatherless guinea pigs running around! Illegitimate guinea pigs, that's what I'd have!

However, in the end, I didn't have the heart to intervene. Who was I to step between two rodents in love? Plus, you should have seen TJ getting ready for her date. Checking herself in the mirror every five minutes, on the phone with her girlfriends all day, writing in her diary about how this was the night she was going to give herself to a complete stranger named Chuck.

Chuck showed up fashionably late, and you should have seen the look on his face. It turned out TJ was three times the size of Chuck, out-weighing him by at least two pounds. It was a Jack Sprat situation if I'd ever seen one. Chuck then had the audacity to look at me as if I were to blame. As if to say, "Hey, man, this isn't the order I placed in my Mail Order Bride catalogue. I ordered Angelina Jolie, not Queen Latifah. You've got exactly five minutes to remedy this situation."

Assuming that guinea pigs are different from humans (but similar to teenagers) we stuck these two random guinea pigs in our backyard and fully expected them to mate. Surely the difficult part of this scenario was over. We had found a female and male guinea pig. Now we would just sit back and wait for babies. It was pretty unfair for us to ignore the social pressure we were putting on these two.

Katie, my wife, put together a delectable salad for TJ and Chuck to enjoy while they got to know each other. You know, to help with the small talk. Plus, they say radishes are an aphrodisiac for guinea pigs. (At least that's what I overheard Chuck explaining to TJ.) The evening progressed as the two of them sat in a grassy spot in the backyard, enjoying their salad and chitchat, all the while trying to ignore the kid paparazzi watching their every move. Sensing that neither TJ nor Chuck were comfortable with their role as exhibitionists, we had the kids come inside the house and we all enjoyed dessert.

Thirty minutes later our friends headed to the backyard to retrieve Chuck and they found him snuggled up next to TJ. Did it take? Did they even try? Had anyone bothered to explain to them how it works? Were they feeling shy? Were they just too full, from the salad?

The gestational period for a guinea pig is 70 days, but I can't wait that long to find out. I'll probably sneak into TJ's room when she's asleep and take a peek at her diary to see if we can expect a whole bunch of little TJs in two months. And then I'll explain to Abbie that of course, we will love the entire litter and raise them as our own. Or auction them off at the ward party, which was how TJ came to our home to begin with.

I realize that despite my strict orders for my children to remain the ages they are now, they are, in fact, going to mature. Or at least get older. Sometimes, in the quiet of a late evening, I feel this foreboding awareness that the sacrifices I will be required to make during the adolescent years will trump anything I've offered up thus far. As a father of a younger brood (ages two years old to 12), perhaps I will actually look back longingly at the moments my sacrifices and service merely required holding a child mid-air as he pooped on my shoes, or venturing into the world of guinea pig mating rituals.

It's possible these parents of teenagers who have spent a great deal of time and energy insisting that I don't understand the emotional endurance I will be required to demonstrate in the face of eye-rolling, independence-flexing, car-driving, hormonal adolescents might be on to something. And then, because all things come full circle, those parents will be expecting that well-deserved apology from me. This time, however, rather than mock them for suggesting I change my egocentric lifestyle for my children, I will most likely be humble enough to offer that apology.

Or another brick to the face.

YOUR LIFE IS AN OCCASION

"Your life is an occasion. Rise to it."

– *Mr. Magorium's Wonder Emporium*

Your Life Is an Occasion

Written August 20, 2012

We occasionally have Movie Night around our house. I kind of like to consider this one of my parenting contributions. Katie has her things; what, with the encouraging morals and values and preparing our children to be valiant, contributing members of society. But when it comes to introducing superheroes, Hobbits, Indiana Jones (with the face melting edited out), or the comical genius of Steve Martin and Martin Short singing "My Little Buttercup"...it's best to just leave that in my hands.

Recently Abbie, my fifteen-year-old, asked if we could watch *Mr. Magorium's Wonder Emporium*. I remember when it came out in theaters; which is saying something, because I don't think it was there for very long. She had already seen it at somebody else's house while babysitting. She'd even asked if we could watch it on a previous Movie Night, but I dismissed it because we needed to watch *Cloudy with a Chance of Meatballs* for a third time, instead.

Having no real defense for not watching it and recognizing that she had been patient when I turned my nose up at it the first time, I agreed.

I was also interested to see why it was that Abbie loved it so. I was hoping maybe it would tell me something about her.

Now, please recognize that I am not recommending this movie to you. I don't know your tastes and this is a quirky movie that is certainly not everyone's cup of Postum. But I will admit that this movie affected me, though in a way that I won't suggest would or should affect everybody. But the stars kind of aligned for me, I guess, and it was a perfect storm.

In a nutshell, here is the story. Natalie Portman plays a 23-year-old musical prodigy, and works for Dustin Hoffman, the Mr. Magorium of said Wonder Emporium, which is essentially a magical wonderland. Now, when Natalie was younger, everyone told her she was a musical genius, a brilliant pianist. That she was special. And she believed them. But now she has grown up and isn't so sure.

There is no mention of Natalie's parents, but Mr. Magorium is somewhat of a father figure to her. And she clearly cares for him, as if she were a daughter. So she is shocked the day that Mr. Magorium tells her that he is "leaving this life." He is not depressed, and this is not about suicide. He has magically lived for more than a hundred years, and it's simply "time to go." He is not upset by this. But whoa-nelly, Natalie sure is! And she is not flattered that he wants to leave the store to her. On the contrary, she believes nobody can or should run the store but him – least of all, her. But before he goes, he gives her this wonderful, inspiring speech wherein he tells her, "Your life is an occasion. Rise to it." He also remarks that she has this *something* in her. This sparkle. This uniqueness that makes her divine. But Natalie still doesn't feel it.

After Mr. M is gone, there's a scene where Natalie and Jason Bateman (who plays the no-nonsense accountant that Mr. Magorium hires to figure out what the store is worth) are in the store, after-hours, alone.

It's quiet, and she stands before Jason and asks him, "When you look at me, what do you see?"

"Really pretty eyes?" he guesses.

And she timidly asks back, "Do you see a sparkle?"

He's confused.

She tries again. "Something reflective of something bigger, trying to get out."

And that's when I felt the lump in my throat.

I'm not exactly sure what that was about, but I believe it had something to do with my daughter. Maybe it's because I could see similarities between Abbie and Natalie's physical features, so I projected Abbie into that situation. Maybe it was because I thought of how Abbie was probably seeing herself in Natalie. Maybe it's because I felt I was watching the story of a father, lovingly wanting to instill this confidence in his daughter, of how incredible and lovely and talented and capable and sparkly and delightful she is…and then to no longer be the prominent male figure in her life, because he is not there and she has grown up… and now she stands before this other man, and in complete vulnerability, asks him if he sees greatness in her. If he recognizes a sparkle. Asking him to validate the feelings and truths that were planted there years before.

And then my favorite part, at the end of the movie (spoiler alert), when Natalie has experienced the needed opportunities to prove to herself that she is all that Mr. Magorium promised her she was, and then – then, Jason Bateman sees the sparkle. Once she believed in herself, the sparkle was evident.

This is what the movie left me quietly reflecting on: I hope that despite my flaws and massive imperfections, my children believe me when I tell them there is greatness in them; that they sparkle. I hope they will remember their childhood and youth as a time they marinated in love. I hope that I am providing the opportunities they need to face experiences that require them to look up, rise up, and walk up; and that when they rise to the occasion, they recognize it. And that whomever they decide to spend their life and eternity with will see the sparkle and enhance it.

~

Take Me Out to the Ballgame

Written April 15, 2006

I have quite an inimitable relationship with baseball. I know the legends of baseball, but I couldn't tell you their statistics. I recognize the names of some major league baseball teams, but I couldn't tell you the name of one, single, major league player. I don't even have a favorite team. But when I attend a baseball game – minor or major league – I feel more patriotic than anything else I do.

Maybe it's the small-town feel that accompanies a minor league game. A sense of a community coming together. Maybe the nostalgia that comes with it since communities are all but non-existent, and "coming together" certainly isn't on their agenda if they do exist. Maybe it's the history of baseball, identified as an American sport, developed at a time when the people of this country were patriotic. They believed in an American dream. They were kinder to each other. Baseball was a commonality between neighbors, cities, states, and the country.

Maybe it's the movies about baseball. Films that use baseball as a backdrop against the protagonist's journey appeal to me on a personal level. I don't know why, really. It's the story of the hero that leaves an impression on me, and not the game of baseball, but somehow the two are intertwined.

Whatever it is about the sport that evokes the emotions that it does in me, they were heightened when my son Garren took an interest in the sport. I came home from work one day, about two years ago, and Garren asked me to play catch with him in the backyard. Garren was four years old at the time and had received a baseball glove from Santa that Christmas.

But to my knowledge, he had never really put it to use, other than using it as a prop as he acted out parts of *The Sandlot*.

I agreed to go play catch with him because he's my son and I love him. Not because I expected a great game of catch. If anything, I expected a great game of "fetch," wherein I would throw the ball, Garren would fetch it, he would "throw" it to me, I would fetch it, and on we would go until dinner was ready.

We walked into the backyard and assumed our posts. I turned and looked at him, waiting there for me to throw the ball. He had his glove up in the air, and a colossal smile on his face. He couldn't wait to play. He looked like the sweetest kid. I threw the ball to him – overhand, even – and, as if the muses of baseball were watching over him, Garren followed the ball with his eyes until he stuck his glove up to meet it. That ball landed right in his glove, with that beautiful echo of a ball hitting a mitt. It was the best sound I had ever heard. Garren was so ecstatic, but so cool about it, he just plucked it out of his glove and threw it back to me. Right back to me. I caught the ball in my glove and threw it back to him. He caught it again. It was no fluke, ladies and gentlemen.

Well, two years later he is finally playing Little League. And my daughter, Abbie, is playing on the same team. She is the only girl on a team of thirteen little hairless boys. If this were a Disney sports movie, she would be the stereotypical female fish-out-of-water character that is at first disregarded by her teammates and dismissed by her coach, only to then impress her coach and teammates with her athletic abilities and woo our hero/team captain with her feminine charm and wily flirtations. Then there's an awkward pre-teen kiss at the end of the movie, after they've pulled together as a team and won the championship.

But we won't be seeing any such kiss at the end of our baseball season. On our first day of practice Abbie ran to second base without getting tagged by the second baseman, who was holding the ball. The first baseman came running over and said, "He won't tag you out ... because he thinks you're hot!" Abbie was recounting this story for me, and judging by her face, she is 23% flattered, 67% offended, and 10% confused by these new feelings.

The week before the first game the coach asked if I would be willing to serve as his Assistant Coach. He singled me out, no doubt, because of my expressed interest in the intricacies of America's greatest pastime, and my unmatched knowledge of the game. You could also argue it might have something to do with him asking, "Are there any parents planning to attend all the games?" at which point I raised my hand and he said, "You, Dad, I need you to be an assistant coach." Then he belched and patted his beer belly. I think we are going to be close friends, Coach Bob and I.

The day of our first game arrived, and we were first up to bat. I took my place on the field as First Base Coach. My job, as it was explained to me, was to stand by First Base and, with league-issued aircraft-landing lights, guide the kids into first base after they hit the ball. I'm kidding of course, my job was never explained to me. Unless you count Coach Bob grunting and pointing at First Base as my explanation. And I do.

I'm not going to lie to you people, my kids are remarkable hitters. Not so much with distance, but with consistency. They have fantastic hand-eye coordination, and as I watched them hit in practice I took comfort in sensing I wouldn't have any anxiety while watching them bat in a game. That is, until they actually played in a game.

My stomach was in knots as the game started. What have I done? Have I set up my children to fail? Have I set them up for public ridicule? Will this single game cause me thousands of dollars in therapy as they grapple with the emotional harm I've incurred upon them at the tender, vulnerable ages of 6 and 8 years old?

My fears were put to rest when Garren stepped up to the plate and immediately knocked out a base hit. He ran up to me at first base and said, "Dad, this is so much fun! Can I play it all year?" He proceeded to run to second, then third. And then Abbie was up to bat. She hit another base hit and ran to first base, while simultaneously allowing her brother to run across home plate. The first run of the season, the first run ever for Garren, made possible by his sister. It will be years before something replaces this moment as one of my Top Favorite Kid Moments.

On the national list of Best First Base Coaches, I'm not sure where I rank. I was stellar at remembering the kids' names, giving them high-fives for making it to first base, and removing their batting helmet and handing it off to the next batter without inappropriately mussing up the kid's hair, as I am wont to do with my own children.

My only weakness made itself known only when my own kid was on the field. Many were the times some kid would hit the ball and instead of making eye contact with him and having him follow me in to first base, I would be yelling at Abbie or Garren to run from second to third, or from third to home. The kid batting was suddenly of no interest to me. It could have been a monkey running to first base.

The kids weren't particularly interested in the score throughout the game, but everyone was excited to have won at the end, a 10 to 4 victory. I felt especially pleased at the outcome. Not necessarily the points, but the fact that my kids felt a little more positive about life, a little more self-assured. Also, because I can now put "First Base Coach" on my resume.

~

Fortysomething

Written March 18, 2013

Me and my dad in Los Angeles ,1971;

the year I was born and he turned 28.

Yesterday was my birthday. (Thank you, and yes, I got your gift. It was just what I wanted! But I got two of them. So, I'm going to return one and use the money to buy some new shoes. But

I'm totally keeping the one you gave me. I'm returning the other guy's gift.)

I am now 42 years old. Not a huge milestone birthday; however, I can confidently report there is no midlife crisis on the horizon. (I check every six months; so, I'm cleared until September.)

I'm actually quite fine being in my 40s. The thing that really stands out to me is being able to so clearly remember when *my dad* was 42. It was 1985. I was 14. My son, Garren, will be 14 this year; the age gap is about the same.

I think about that decade for my dad and me. Ten years of milestones or rites of passage for me, all while my dad was in his 40s.

In 1983 I started junior high school, became a deacon, and received the Aaronic Priesthood. I think I also started officially using deodorant and loved watching *The Outsiders*. And my dad turned 40.

In 1985 I started high school, began attending early-morning seminary, went on week-long Scouting high adventures, played on the high school water polo team...and my dad was in his 40s.

From 1987 to 1988 I became a priest, started driving, started dating, had my first kiss, got my first and second speeding tickets, went to my first U2 concert, went on a week-long surfing trip to Ensenada, Mexico, moved to Hawaii with my family, went skydiving...and my dad was in his 40s.

1989 to 1990 I had graduated high school, started college at BYU, received the Melchizedek Priesthood, and left on a mission to Portugal... and my dad was in his 40s.

In 1992 I came home from my mission and started back up at college… and my dad was in his 40s.

I am sure my dad experienced new things and had his own life alterations during his 40s, but for an egocentric teenager, it seemed like my world changed a thousand times over, and all while my dad was in his 40s. My dad will be 70 this year; but somewhere in my mind, he will always be in his 40s. And that's the decade I am in now. And for some reason, *that* is what kind of blows my mind.

The Former Bishop

Written August 27, 2012

2 Timothy 4:6-7 For ... the time of my departure is at hand. I have fought a good fight, I have finished my course, I have kept the faith.

Yesterday I was released as bishop of the Elk Ridge Ward, in the Elkhorn Springs Stake in The Church of Jesus Christ of Latter-day Saints.

I had served for 5 years and about three months. Which sounds like a long time, and it is; but mulling over countless memories, June 2007 just doesn't seem that long ago. My hair color says different.

This was me in 2007.

And this is me in 2012.

Just kidding.

This is me and Katie, yesterday. August 26, 2012. And yes, that may be more salt than pepper.

In those five years I turned 40 (last year), had two children (technically, Katie had them, in the verb sense of things), dabbled in three different careers, traveled to China, Brazil, and all over the U.S. of A., contributed as an author to a book I'm proud of, started a business, bought a 12-passenger van, and lost 10 lbs.

I also had the honor of having a front-row seat to thousands of miracles and tender mercies. But those aren't my stories to tell. It was just a privilege to be invited and trusted to be there.

It seems understood and accepted among members of the Church that a bishop sacrifices many hours a week, giving up time with family, work, hobbies, or rest, in order to serve. And yes, there are moments of profound heartache and sadness and wishing you could instantly make things better for somebody.

But...but... there are moments when heaven is touching earth, and you are standing on hallowed ground as you sit with somebody in their home or in a room at the church building or the temple or at a campsite or traveling in a car – and you feel the divinity of that person, and how loved they are by an Eternal Father. And you promise yourself in that moment that you will never forget that feeling. And you feel bonded to that person in a way that you hope makes you friends forever.

I am grateful for those moments. They have changed me and I will miss them.

~

Alone Again, Unnaturally

Written June 25, 2009

Do you ever bask in the adorableness of your children and thank your lucky stars that our world is so ethically shallow as to actually cater to good-looking people – because it means your children have a bright future? Me too.

Katie and the kids left earlier this week to visit some of our lovely extended family members, who are both lovely and extended. And I will be joining them at a later date. It has left me alone for a few days. I miss them. And with all that silence, I have felt reflective. Well, that's not what I felt first, obviously. No, first I felt the freedom of treating my house like it was the studio for a Men's Underwear photo shoot, featuring me (and only me). Then I felt the freedom of eating an unjustifiable amount of Haagen-Dazs ice cream. Then I felt the freedom of watching far too many reruns of *Seinfeld* (I hadn't before realized there was such a thing.) And then I felt the freedom of a house so eerily quiet, I could hear the fruit ripening on our pear tree. Outside.

And then I realized how seldom in my life I have been home alone, and how lonely an empty house is. And I felt reflective....

I was lounging in the bathroom the moment I found out I was going to be a dad for the first time. We were at my parents' house, and it was Thanksgiving. Everybody had finished dinner, and we excused ourselves as we snuck off to the bathroom so Katie could pee on a stick. Also so she could take a home pregnancy test. (Zoing! Thank you, I'll be here all week! Don't forget to tip your waitress!)

I will forever remember Katie's face when she held up that little stick with the two lines. We stared at each other in complete silence, but the moment was emotionally deafening. I was thrilled and overwhelmed. Confident and vulnerable. In love and uncertain. I cried. Katie cried. There was fluid from every orifice. Me, my wife, and a baby – feeling our lives change while hanging out in a bathroom. (I had no idea in that instant how prevalent the bathroom and babies would be in our future.)

Each time one of my six children have been born, I have felt this inherent tug inside me to say something so profound – so thought provoking and weighty – that every communication medium in the world would shove a microphone in my face and ask me to repeat my brilliant insight so it could serve as the perfect sound bite for what joy feels like. But the words have never come. And they never do, not even in the small non-life-altering moments.

Like that first time you come home from work and your baby recognizes that it's YOU and that you are somehow very important to them and you have been gone, and they squeal and their little body shakes until you hold them. I love that.

Like when you watch your child timidly attempt something far removed from their comfort zone, but they exercise the hope and trust, even faith, that they will succeed, and it will be fun or rewarding or wonderful. And then it is. Like when your young, inhibited son, who hesitates to ever openly demonstrate confidence completely destroys the competition in a half-mile race.

Or when your 11-year old writes a poem for you for Fathers' Day that is so personal and sweet and loving that publishing it publicly would belittle it.

Or when your daughter tells you that she wants to marry somebody just like you.

Or when you leave the house for two minutes to get the mail and when you come back in the house your three-year-old cocks his head to the side, as if he's just read a chapter out of How to Look so Adorable Your Parents Will Give you Anything, and says, "Dad. When you were gone, I missed you."

Or when your daughter refuses to ever let you leave the house without giving you a hug and a kiss. Or when your children don't know you are watching them, and they are just being their unguarded selves, and it is like watching lyrics being written.

My hope – and I have to believe this is true – is that in the Next Life, at our leisure, we are able to instantaneously recall each mortal moment, and almost relive it. That we will be able to readily bring to memory all of these moments. Moments that affected you in a way that you just couldn't attach words to.

I also have to believe that in the Next Life, Haagen-Dazs is served upon your arrival. That's just good hospitality.

~

Personal Legacy

Written July 22, 2013

When we speak of Latter-day Saint Pioneers, we can't help but speak reverently of their legacy of sacrifice and devotion. I, myself, am a descendant of John Tanner. John was an entrepreneurial kind of a guy. He owned several farms and orchards, as well as a hotel in upstate New York. He received an impression that he was needed in Kirtland, Ohio – so he sold those farms and orchards and that hotel, and packed up his family Christmas morning to head 500 miles east to Kirtland. When he got there, he found the mortgage on the temple site was due. He loaned money to the temple committee and to the Prophet Joseph Smith, personally. He then donated liberally to the cause. When he left Kirtland, he had $7.50 to his name. Years later, in Nauvoo, he was called at the age of 66 to serve a mission. Leaving his wife and 14 children, he was on his way out of town when he passed the prophet. Joseph said, "John, what of the $2,000 I owe you?" John responded, "It's yours. You owe me nothing." The prophet put his hand on John's shoulder and said, "Bless you, Brother Tanner. Your posterity will never beg for bread."

Many times in my life I have been the recipient of that promised blessing. As a child, as a husband, and as a father. And inevitably, I reflectively ask myself what I will be known for by my posterity.

I mean, you have to wonder what kind of legacy you are leaving for your children when they make astute observations like, "I can't wait to be a dad – you get to stay up every night eating ice cream and watching TV!" Apparently, I have painted quite a picture of fatherhood for my three sons. "Yep, that's all there is to it, my boys! You put in your time as a youth spending grueling hours making forts out of the couch and playing Wipeout on the Wii; and then in a few short years, you'll be living the high life with Haagen-Dazs and *Seinfeld* reruns. Life just gets simpler and simpler, I tell you."

What kind of legacy would I like to leave my children? Oh, I suppose I'd like them to say ...

My dad was the wisest person I ever knew.

My dad could solve any problem.

He never said a bad word about anyone.

He was the most patient man in the entire world.

I remember when he made his first $1M at age 43. (Next year!)

My mom always commented on how great he looked in a medium t-shirt.

However, my flaws and selfish indulgences are incessantly on parade at my house. It's difficult to hide them when there are seven pairs of eyes watching. Somebody is always seeing something. So, if you were to ask my children this afternoon how they would remember me…for better or for worse, it might realistically sound more like this:

My dad was do-it-yourself-home-repair-challenged and he hyphenated words far too often.

He knew a little too much about a lot of 80s and 90s pop-culture.

He couldn't tell you the name of a single player of any professional sport.

He was his most impatient when we were whiny, which he always said was an expression of ingratitude.

My dad valued friendship. Especially mine.

He loved telling stories.

He could not dance or sing, but he loved dancing and singing with me.

I knew how to make more meals than my dad.

My dad was honest.

I felt emotionally and physically safe with him.

Though imperfectly, he tried all his life to be a better follower of the Savior.

More than anything else, my dad loved my mom.

Epilogue

Written July 21, 2019

According to Wikipedia – where I get all my news – (well, that and IMDB) – Albert Einstein's theory of relativity explains the law of gravitation and its relation to other forces of nature. It applies to the cosmological and astrophysical realm, including astronomy.

I have no idea what I just wrote. I'm no Einstein, you guys.

Fortunately, our ol' pal, Albert, also explained it this way: Put your hand on a hot stove for a minute, and it seems like an hour. Sit with a pretty girl for an hour, and it seems like a minute. That's relativity.

Thanks for dumbing it down for me, Al.

Relatively speaking, it feels like the last five years have zipped by, each year perpetually increasing in speed. It's been said that the fastest thing on land is the cheetah. Have you heard that? That's actually incorrect. The fastest thing on land – and this is a proven fact – is 2014 to 2019.

Katie and I got married in 1995 and started having children in 1997. From 1997 to 2013, it was the era of baby-making, wherein we made eight babies. (I apologize for the use of scientific jargon.) That's a long era. And it became so familiar, it seemed it would never end. Like the Ice Age, or *Friends*. Years passed, but there were constants. There were so many things that always looked and sounded and felt the same – and it gave me the false sense that it would always be that way.

There was always somebody that wanted to be held. There were always first words and toothless kisses. There was youthful giddiness about holidays and costumes and presents and food. There were always mealtimes when we were all together. There was storytelling and the birth of inside jokes. And at the end of the night, Katie and I would sit down with bowls of ice cream to watch a show … and all the people we made were safely gathered in and sleeping in their beds. The world was quiet, and the people I loved the most were nearby. Happy.

It was the era of my nucleus family.

I'm not naïve. And this isn't a revisionist history of that era. Not everything was easy or perfect. There was crying and ingratitude and lying. There were fits and tempers lost. There were inconveniences and interruptions. There were financial setbacks and desperate prayers when there were no clear paths or foreseeable safety nets. And there was expensive electronic equipment casually broken by toddlers.

I'm also not sad about my family growing up and changing. I've loved going to Marvel movie premiers. I've loved river rafting and hiking Angels Landing with my teenagers. I've loved watching my children navigate friendships and relationships. I've loved going to the temple with my children and worshiping with them. I've loved falling in love with people they love. I've loved the manifestations of their own personalities, strengths, and interests. I've loved seeing them mature in spiritual, educational, and civic areas.

I think what surprises me and what I feel most sensitive to – is how brief mortality is. How quickly time passes. That era that seemed to last forever is not only over, but this next era, instead of keeping pace, acts like it's on a "people mover" at the airport. Hey, what's your hurry, new era?

This year has especially punctuated the speed of life. Maybe it's because my dad unexpectedly and suddenly passed away in April. Maybe it's because my daughter got married this month and is starting her own family. Maybe it's because I have a son currently living out of the country, serving a mission in Brazil for The Church of Jesus Christ of Latter-day Saints. Maybe it's because I'm not totally confident of how frequently we'll all be in the same room from now on. Maybe it's because my youngest is 5, and we've never had a youngest at 5. But lately, I feel hyper-aware of the people in my life and the commodity of time. Everyone and everything keep changing. And so quickly. I love who they are, and who they continue to become. And at the same time, I feel like I spend some portion of each day trying to recapture memories ... sorting them and making sure they're all still there.

It has certainly heightened my emotions. I am not depressed or melancholy. I am thrilled with how much happiness abounds in my life. But my emotions are inevitably and constantly near the surface, and tears come at the most random occasions.

These are good things. Just bigger things. Things requiring more faith and more hope. More emotional chutzpah. Because in this era, I am more uncertain of what next month and next year will look like.

I feel profound gratitude. Overwhelming appreciation. Consuming love. Awareness of goodness. Also, I miss my dad. My heart goes out to my mom. I miss the eras gone by. I worry that I'm not clutching each moment – and yet I realize how fleeting each instant is, and how impossible it would be to mark them all. And how obnoxious I would be if I attempted it.

Sometime back, Katie and I watched this quiet little movie, *Still Mine*. I don't know if anyone else in the world has seen it. A married couple in their 80s decides to build a smaller house on their property in the northeast, so it's easier for them to get around. The movie is peppered with scenes where they reflect on life together, and in one scene, the husband recalls a dining room table he'd built. It got to me.

"The first few years, every nick that table absorbed, I took it personally. It was all I could see. The dent from a fork, the scratch from a skate blade, the ghost of someone's handwriting, pressed through a piece of paper. There were a lot of times I regretted not making that table out of oak. But as the years went by and the scars added up ... the imperfections turned that table into something else. That's the thing about pine. It holds a lot of memories."

I'm not that savvy with wood. But I've been a dad long enough that when I heard that sentiment ... I felt like I understood it. It affected me. The changes in perspective that come with experience. I'm grateful for the "pine" in my life. For the memories held, for the imperfections that make my life "something else." Something I couldn't have designed on my own. I'm grateful for the privilege of being a husband and being a dad. For being surrounded by people who are generous enough to point out the good and forgive the less-than-good. I am grateful for the moments.

This collection of stories stands as my attempt to capture some of those moments. The moments that become part of that pine table that is the culture of our family. And it should be read while eating ice cream. Of this I am sure.

Made in the USA
Columbia, SC
27 November 2019